ENDLESS DEPTHS

Essays on Cosmic Themes, Weird Lore, & Hidden Knowledge

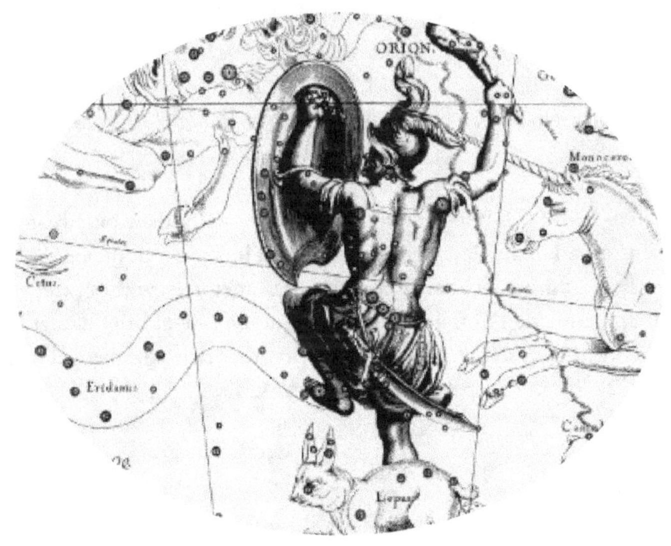

ALECO JULIUS

FORBIDDEN DOOR
PRESS

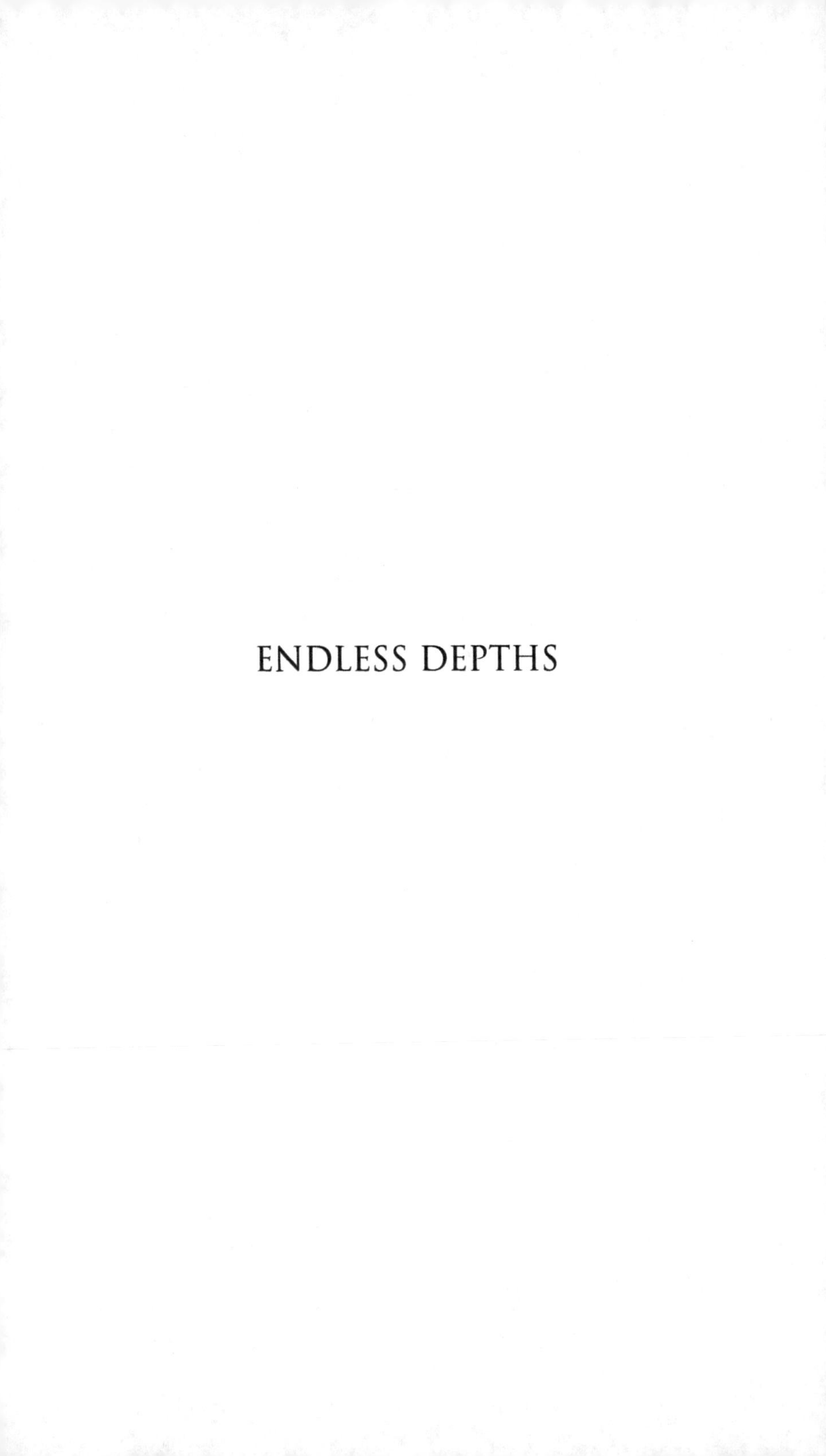

ENDLESS DEPTHS

For My Father

"Consciousness is much more than the thorn, it is the dagger in the flesh."

E.M. Cioran

"Everything under the sun is in tune, but the sun is eclipsed by the moon."

Pink Floyd

TABLE OF CONTENTS

INTRODUCTION

Thank you for picking up this book. Know that I appreciate your interest and support of a book whose topics are diverse and obscure.

Truly, the book is a mere slice of my lifelong pursuit of the type of knowledge that Agent Dale Cooper of *Twin Peaks* would call "both wonderful and strange." The publications in which most of these essays have originally appeared are the most wonderful and strange imaginable, and I am proud to have contributed to each.

I encourage you to take a look at the table of contents and peruse what might interest you. In that sense, the pieces do not have to be read in order. Skip around, read an essay, take a break, pick it back up when you're in the mood to delve into something wonderful and strange to balance out a particularly mundane day.

Traverse the threshold of the forbidden door.

-AJ

1

<hr>

The Abyss of All Being

In June of 1788, in a small boat on the North Sea, Scottish geologist James Hutton and two other men gazed towards the craggy shore. As they looked upon Siccar Point, on the east coast of Scotland, they were left with conflicting emotions. The exposed promontory was composed of two rock types, vertical greywacke and horizontal red sandstone-- a geological clash between lithic forms that would prove symbolic of an impending internal conflict within the aggregate nineteenth-century consciousness.

Earlier that morning, Hutton and his two companions had embarked from Edinburgh on an excursion to seek out evidence of his lifelong theory: that the earth was far more ancient than anyone had yet fathomed. For years, Hutton had intuited that land was formed by cycles of erosion, sedimentation, and uplift. The example of unconformity at Siccar Point represents two separate cycles, where each rock type was created by the commonplace forces of the earth, such as rain, waves, wind, earthquakes, and volcanoes.

The land under our feet, surmised Hutton, was the product of a world machine that broke itself down and built itself back up in cycles of unimaginable duration.

Juxtaposed rock formations that were unique in makeup and strata suggested that the cycles of natural history were only possible with the availability of an immense amount of time, a period of time that is all but incomprehensible to the human mind. Hutton had guessed correctly that, due to the relentless pounding of the elements upon the North Sea coast, there would be exposed rock offering a glimpse of the land's deep past. One of his two companions on that June day was John Playfair, friend, protégé, and future biographer. He later wrote about this exultant moment at Siccar Point:

An epocha still more remote presented itself, when even the most ancient of the rocks [...] was not yet disturbed by that immeasurable force which has burst asunder the solid pavement of the globe. Revolutions still more remote appeared in the distance of this extraordinary perspective. The mind seemed to grow giddy by looking so far into the abyss of time.

Hutton's theory was in sharp contrast to most models of land formation at that time, which posited instead that catastrophic events had suddenly and dramatically transformed the world's topography. In 1785, three years before his consequential boat trip, Hutton delivered two key lectures to the Royal Society of Edinburgh. He discussed a measure of time that far surpassed notions of prevailing temporality, eventually becoming the concept of deep time. This geological framework was necessarily much vaster than the alleged mere thousands of years in current vogue.

He ended his lecture with: "The result, therefore, of our present enquiry is, that we find no vestige of a beginning, -no prospect of an end."

The Royal Society apparently took his theory of deep time into consideration but did not exactly embrace it. The book based on his lectures, *The Theory of the Earth,* was not printed for another three years. Most notably, German geologist Abraham Gottlob Werner, along with an acolyte, were unyieldingly antagonistic towards Hutton. They took their opposition to almost villainous heights, methodically opposing him to gain notoriety.

Hutton's previous studies in other fields were essential to his ultimate theory. During the 1740s at Edinburgh, he studied Newton's theories of universal gravitation and planetary motion. Eminent paleontologist Stephen Jay Gould notes that Newton's work had expanded space, while Hutton's work had expanded time. Soon thereafter, while searching for his niche in the hastening Scottish Enlightenment period, Hutton earned his medical degree from Leiden University.

Significantly, his thesis was called *The Blood and the Circulation of the Microcosm.* The title suggests a parallelism between the human body's circulatory system and the solar system—the microcosm and the macrocosm. Hutton made this connection clear in the 1795 edition of *Theory of the Earth*:

All the surface of this earth is formed according to a regular system of heights and hollows, hills and valleys, rivulets and rivers, and these rivers return the waters of the atmosphere into the general mass, in like manner as the blood, returning to the heart, is conducted in the veins.

For Gould, the immensity of deep time is so powerfully inconceivable to the human mind that it can only be understood as a metaphor. But could the above passage be dismissed as metaphor only? Or did Hutton strike upon the idea, after rigorous work in physics and biology, that the earth is a kind of living entity whose cycles clearly obey the laws of the universe both micro and macro? These are the questions that Hutton would contemplate and cultivate for years to come. And the British landscape would be his laboratory.

A Petrifying New Reality

To nineteenth-century spectators of natural history, the idea of deep time was intensely revolutionary. Models of earth's history had been written for centuries, but were examples of biblical geology. In the eyes of the church, these systems were meant to be conclusive, while challenges to the status quo were dealt with severely.

At the First Council of Nicaea (325CE), Eusebius attempted an early chronology going back to the Book of Genesis. Church doctors Augustine (354-430CE) and Albertus Magnus (c.1200-1280) reportedly found fossils such as a petrified dinosaur egg and a mammoth tooth. They interpreted these discoveries as sourced by antediluvian giants, always in adherence to the doctrine of biblical narrative scope. As written in Genesis, an arcane race of prodigious beings known as the Nephilim roamed the earth before Noah's Flood. They purportedly existed alongside other enormous creatures, such as the Book of Job's Behemoth and Leviathan.

Fossils of the earth's extinct megafauna fed the mythologies of these giants for centuries. Scholar and Primate of All Ireland James Ussher confidently determined in 1650 that the earth was created in October of 4004 B.C. Theologian Thomas Burnet's *The Sacred Theory of the Earth* (1681) was even admired by Isaac Newton and Edmond Halley for its erudition and philosophical rigor.

In essence, the discovery of deep time was the reckoning of a new reality which revealed profound, deep-rooted anxieties in the popular consciousness. Thirty-six years after Hutton's 1788 boat trip, his second companion, fellow naturalist James Hall, would personally take the young geologist Charles Lyell to Siccar Point, so that he, too, might look for himself so far into the abyss of time. Lyell was converted to Huttonianism for life. The impact of Lyell's 1830 book *The Principles of Geology* was congealed when it was lauded by Charles Darwin, who regarded Lyell as instrumental to his own theory of natural selection.

The time revolution exposed the suppressed baseness of proto-humanity, and contrasted with the Victorian adherence to civilized respectability. Just when the seeds of modern industrialization had been planted, it seemed, the earth began to yield its old secrets. Although the avowed enlightened progress of science was encouraging society to rise from a barbarian past, it was simultaneously confronted by a new petrifying reality-- and with it, its own all-too-clear triviality. The burgeoning popularity of archeology in Britain was enhancing knowledge of human prehistory, yet Hutton's discovery of deep time threatened to render the totality of human history entirely insignificant.

Ecologist Jeffrey Jerome Cohen writes that society suffered an "ontological vertigo" which reverberated through the century.

The early nineteenth century also curated the birth and development of paleontology. William Smith, often called the father of English geology, in 1815 had created the first detailed map of the British underground. Fossil-hunting became fieldwork for the natural philosopher as well as a hobby for the amateur Victorian. Unlike the church doctors, paleontologists realized that fossils were the remnants of extinct organisms. Was the human race also susceptible to this unthinkable fate?

A fossil recently reexamined by the British Geological Survey, originally found on the nineteenth century Jurassic coast, is a veritable metaphor for the long temporal reach of obscure eldritch terror. In the fossil, a primitive fish has met its brutal fate, forever persevered within an early cephalopod's tentacular embrace. In addition to Victorian worries of uncontrollable impulses that might arise from the depths of the body-mind construct, they now had to contend with the seismic weight of another dreadful prospect: human extinction. Nineteenth century scholar Aaron Worth writes that the revelation of deep time forced a "new conceptual space to [emerge], itself representing a powerful, collective act of integration."

This integration was negotiated in literature by authors such as Arthur Machen, Algernon Blackwood, and H.G. Wells. One noteworthy story that explored the terror of deep time is Machen's *The Great God Pan*, a work fraught with primeval undertones. In it, a mysterious character named Helen, ostensible offspring of Pan, experiences a strange death. Her body transforms between beast and human, female and male, before resting as an amorphous gelatinous substance. Machen's language is conspicuously similar to that of John Playfair: "[I saw] the body descend to the beasts whence it ascended, and that which was on the heights go down to the depths, even to the abyss of all being."

Machen's work was in part a revelation of nineteenth century fears of a concealed savage hybridity within our organic forms. Worth asserts that "*Pan* is emblematic of the culturally repressed act of integration," representative of the maddening incomprehensibly of geological time. Thence, from Helen's death came the birth of modern cosmic horror.

A generation later, H.P. Lovecraft further preyed upon the fears of the primordial unknown, establishing deep time as a trope of weird literature. He wrote in the story "The Shadow Out of Time," for instance, of "monstrous unguessable horrors" out of the "seething vortex of time," whereby humanity must accept its own place in the cosmos, however paralyzing. Interestingly, Gould has called ancient fossilized organisms the Old Ones, in reference to Lovecraft's pantheon of ancient alien deities buried within the earth, as seen in *At the Mountains of Madness*.

Nature writer Robert Macfarlane has called attention to the fact that the word *humanity* has roots in the word *humus*, meaning soil, earth, or ground. Over vast amounts of time, the earth folds, shifts, gouts, transforms, and absorbs. Like the earth, there is a geology of the body-- the mineralization of calcium into bones, and the rivers of blood within our flesh.

Deep time is embedded within us, and it cannot be escaped. Macfarlane also writes that deep time opens into the future as well as the past. Exactly how humanity will react to the terrifying gulf ahead remains to be seen.

Sources

Derleth, August, ed. *The Best of H.P. Lovecraft.* Del Rey, 1982.

Gould, Stephen Jay. *Time's Arrow, Time's Cycle: Myth and Metaphor in the Discovery of Geological Time.* Harvard, 1987.

Macfarlane, Robert. *Underland: A Deep Time Journey.* W.W. Norton, 2019.

Repcheck, Jack. *The Man Who Found Time: James Hutton and the Discovery of the Earth's Antiquity.* Basic Books, 2003.

Stone, Jeffrey Jerome. *Stone: An Ecology of the Inhuman.* University of Minnesota, 2015.

Winchester, Simon. *The Map That Changed the World: William Smith and the Birth of Modern Geology.* Harper Perennial, 2001.

Woodward, Aylin. "Stunning Fossil Reveals Brutal Squid Attack From 200 Million Years Ago." Science Alert, 11 May 2020. https://www.sciencealert.com/evidence-of-a-200-million-year-old-squid-attack-was-frozen-in-time. Accessed 13 Jan. 2021.

Worth, Aaron. "Arthur Machen and the Horrors of Deep History." *Victorian Literature and Culture*, vol. 40, no. 1, 2012, pp. 215–227., www.jstor.org/stable/41413829. Accessed 30 Jan. 2021.

2

STRANGERS IN THIS WORLD

In a letter dated July 1888, Vincent van Gogh wrote to his brother: "Why, I wonder, should the shining points of the heavens be less accessible to us than the dots on a map?" This question was posed two years before he died of a self-inflicted gunshot wound. In those last two years of his life, van Gogh's production was fiendishly prolific. He was at times averaging more than a painting per day. This output included series of works in which he repeatedly painted the same tree or flower in an ostensible attempt to understand it, to somehow dig into the heart of its meaning.

Becoming an artist, van Gogh believed, was akin to taking holy orders. His continual reach for the profundity of nature exhausted him in the end. Whether or not he thought there would ever be a finality to his work, capturing nature's essence in its totality always seemed just beyond the horizon. His painting was more than an obsession; it was more like a state of possession.

The shapes and forms of nature that appear on his canvases are phantasms in a liminal space, a window between the worlds of outside reality and his own mind.

Simultaneously, another individual was conducting his own search for the nature of reality. Though the late nineteenth century abounded with novel scientific theories in all manner of fields, physicist Ludwig Boltzmann had his thoughts trained on the forces of existence. Much of his work described the phenomena of subatomic particles, which were in his era still a doubtful theory in the eyes of many scientists. He is known for his entropy equation, which in a nutshell proves that energy tends to spread out. It explains why ice cubes melt when taken out of the freezer, or why hot coffee cools down rather than heats up.

Entropy also explains why the oxygen molecules are all spread throughout a room. If they were to suddenly cluster in the corner near the ceiling, you would suffocate. So, when given the opportunity, energy spreads out evenly. Boltzmann recognized that there was no magic involved, no conscious entity guiding the energy of the universe toward some substantial goal, but a physical principle. Little by little, it seemed as though Divinity's grip on 19th-century society was slowly being replaced by physics. This was the apprehension of scientists as well as artists, and all thinking people in between. Known as a kind and generous family man, Boltzmann nevertheless incessantly searched for new knowledge. A colleague of his called him "a stranger in this world." Boltzmann hanged himself in 1906 at the age of 62.

Both Van Gogh and Boltzmann loved to be out in nature. Van Gogh often took his easel out into the wild to paint, capturing open fields and towering trees under expanses of open sky. His paintings were measures of particular mornings, afternoons, and evenings. Sometimes the sun bore down with intensity, and sometimes the gray sky rained. The severe rapidity with which he worked developed over his brief ten-year career, so that in the end he was "doing violence to form," in the words of his brother Theo.

In this way did his painting become less like realism and more an abstract distortion. Writing about the work of Boltzmann, contemporary physicist Eric Johnson declares that "our powers of abstraction will be much greater here than the powers of our senses." This point makes sense if one considers that subatomic particles cannot be seen or felt. Rather, the imagination must be fully put to use in order to comprehend the impossibly enormous number of particles that reside in your bedroom alone. Imagination, therefore, was a vital tool in the crafting of Boltzmann's entropy equation, just as it was for Van Gogh in crafting his famous sunflowers. Still, Boltzmann was fond of appealing to his senses with visits to the seaside. In fact, it was at a coastal Italian village on the Adriatic Sea that he took his own life. Did he travel there with his family, knowing it would be his last vista?

In his scientific work, Boltzmann was able to give future physicists permission, so to speak, to use their mind's eye in their search for the nature of reality. By this measure did he possess a mind similar to that of the painter. This is not to say that his work was fantasy-- it was upheld by rigorous standards. Similarly, Van Gogh's own high standards compelled him to clearly paint what his mind's eye perceived. Art historian Ingo F. Walther writes that he "had always been reaching for infinity." This is the kind of spirit that early science fiction author Jules Verne championed in his literature around the same period. Although the limits of science and the limits of art might seem to have led to opposing directions, both Boltzmann and Van Gogh relentlessly pursued the most enigmatic knowledge of the natural world.

Van Gogh's goal was to peer intensely into nature and capture its spirit on the canvas. Walther states that Van Gogh's dream had been to paint the harmony of "spatial dimensions," yet ended up in its "vertiginous depths." In one of his multitudinous, deftly-written letters, Van Gogh claims that "Nature has spoken to me." Boltzmann, too, focused his attention toward the boundaries of the knowable. Even as he gained an ever deeper understanding of the quantum universe, he shifted toward philosophical questions. It was not enough for Boltzmann to know how physics worked, but *why*. These forays into the meanings of nature resulted in a great loneliness in each of these figures.

In their inexorable search to know, Van Gogh and Boltzmann became strangers to the world, as the latter's colleague had observed. This is evident in Van Gogh's dysfunctional relationships, from his tumultuous time living with a prostitute to the disastrous ending of his acquaintance with the artist Paul Gaugin. Similarly, Boltzmann had ruined his own appointment to a prestigious professorship in Berlin with his social awkwardness, his indecision, and his inability to read the tone of certain formal situations. Van Gogh wrote of his "divine sadness," a condition which he thought affected no one outside himself.

In turn, Boltzmann may have had a difficult time relating to others whose intellects were simply not of his ilk.

During their lifetimes, the work of both painter and physicist were not met with the most success in the eyes of others. Van Gogh sold exactly one painting during his lifetime. The importance of Boltzmann's equation was not truly appreciated until long after his death. According to Walther, Van Gogh's mind drifted toward believing that "if his work was worth nothing, then he too must be worth nothing." Near the end, he suffered bouts of mental illness. He tried to ingest paint, for instance, not to mention the famed ear-cutting incident. Boltzmann suffered from what in modern times we would call severe anxiety and possibly depression. In a book of lectures, Boltzmann wrote: "I am conscious of being only an individual struggling weakly against the stream of time."

What truths did these men see in the abyssal spaces of existence? If we follow the arrow of time into the deep future, we see that all systems of the universe will eventually dissolve into chaos. Boltzmann's equation helps to explain how energy will disperse to the point of extreme entropy, an equilibrium in which all matter degrades, and therefore advent the slow death of all things. One of Van Gogh's late paintings was "The Starry Night," in which shining points of the heavens are suspended among the swirling dark. In the end, the painter made them his own, and accessible to all who endeavor to look deeply.

Epilogue

The afterlife of the work of Vincent Van Gogh is a continuing crescendo. Retrospectives and exhibitions of his work are of course attended by the multitudes. Immense credit for this popularity is due to the painter's sister-in-law Johanna Van Gogh-Bonger, who tirelessly worked to bring attention to the artwork. During his lifetime, he wanted his paintings to be seen. Today, they are imprinted upon the fabric of the entire world as commodities of global pop culture. You can find his paintings on hoodies and baseball caps as well as refrigerator magnets and shower curtains.

As for Ludwig Boltzmann, his place in the development of physics is rightfully recognized. We must wonder whether he would have been amused or perturbed that is name is attached to the bewildering Boltzmann Brain hypothesis, which posits that your consciousness is merely a random collection of particles that spontaneously formed in a void. The idea is that it is more likely for a brain to have abruptly appeared than the developed order of the universe. This means that all your memories, sensations, and desires are false illusions. Even, and especially, your current thoughts.

Bibliography

Johnson, Eric. *Anxiety and the Equation: Understanding Boltzmann's Entropy.* MIT Press, 2018.

Walther, Ingo F. *Van Gogh: The Complete Paintings.* Taschen, 1993.

3

ENDLESS FORMS MOST BEAUTIFUL

Imagine for a moment: A clear bright afternoon in a garden yard of vibrant green. A young poet sits under the canopy of a sprawling mulberry tree. Something about this tree has a vague connection to the ideas that have been coalescing in the young poet's heart—epic ideas about creation. The year is 1625, and John Milton is in his first year at Christ's College, Cambridge. The image of the mulberry tree above him takes root inside him, and grows over time. Eventually, as his life changes, this image manifests forty years later as the Tree of the Knowledge of Good and Evil, which he plants as the fulcrum around which he spins his classic epic poem *Paradise Lost*.

This is, of course, a leap of the imagination, although all the foundations for an intriguing bit of lore are here. A mulberry tree is still there to this day in the Fellows' Garden, a scion of the tree planted in the spot in 1609. It truly is a wonderful natural monument. Its abundantly full branches and leaves reach up and out, commanding its own section of the garden.

Having weathered storms and the ravages of time, it is now propped up by wooden posts. Interestingly, Milton himself was born in 1608, and the closeness of his birth and the planting of the tree solidified the naming of the mulberry after him.

In the early years of the seventeenth century, King James I of England wished to compete with other European nations in the prosperous silk trade. In order to start his own silk industry, he ordered the planting of thousands of mulberries around the country, the trees' leaves being the silkworm's primary food. The silkworm, which is actually a caterpillar, lives off the tree and creates a cocoon of raw silk. However, the king's plan did not quite work out. As was to be discovered, the silkworms tended to prefer the leaves of the white mulberry tree, whereas England was populated with the black variety. Furthermore, the British weather is reported to have had too harsh an effect on the tree's leaves to effectively support the silkworm.

As transformation plays a central role in the life cycle of the silkworm, so it does in my own part of this story. I had hoped to someday pilgrimage to Milton's Mulberry ever since I had first heard of its existence. It occupied a sort of mystical place in my imagination. Although I can scarcely articulate why, I felt a thread connecting me to it, and that I needed to reach it in the flesh to complete a kind of personal quest. Not that it was at the forefront of my thoughts, but each time I read *Paradise Lost,* a vague mental image of the mulberry would appear as a reminder. I was introduced to Milton's epic poem in my youth by a teacher with an infectious enthusiasm, and I was instantly enamored. Certainly, I did not understand everything that Milton offered in the poem at first read, and I still discover secrets each time I read it. At the time, I let the words of the poem wash over me, and I have not forgotten that early intoxication. It occurred to me that the poem contained a magic that was real, right there in its words and language, reaching out to me across the ages.

Eventually, the reading of *Paradise Lost* led me to a career in literature and a lifelong love of the written word. As time went on, I realized that a core idea in the poem is the same idea that most attracts me to any kind of literature—the idea that Milton's masterpiece is in itself a theodicy, an attempt to explain the problem of evil in the world. The poem's window into God's mind and Satan's motivations gives us a representation of eternal conflict, one that masterfully intertwines a fictional narrative with religious scripture. We even get to witness the birth of Death itself. The problem of evil goes hand in hand with the problem of human suffering, which I argue is the core idea that the roads of great literature lead us to. In Milton's view, the creation of the world is founded on a conflict of epic scale, one that has never ceased reverberating through generations of humanity and time and, indeed, plays itself out in large and small ways each day. Milton's poem was his exhibition of the logical problem of evil and suffering in the world, juxtaposed with the wonder and beauty that proceeds from the will of the Creator. He writes, "The Earth obeyed, and straight opening her fertile womb teemed at a birth innumerous living creatures, perfect forms."

Two centuries later, these ideas would be recapitulated by another man in the shadow of the mulberry tree bearing Milton's name. Charles Darwin had spent a few years at Christ's College before heeding the call of the sea and the continents beyond. Born 201 years after Milton, Darwin trod the same grounds at the same age in his life. Anyone who studies at this school knows the lore of Milton's Mulberry, and it delights the imagination to think about the ways the poet inspired Darwin. In fact, the connection between the two men is well documented. Darwin himself proclaimed that he carried a copy of *Paradise Lost* with him aboard HMS *Beagle*, and on excursions ashore, he said, if he could only afford to carry one book, Milton's would be it.

Originally, Darwin planned to become a clergyman, but his five-year voyage throughout the world transformed him into the lifelong naturalist we remember him as today. The journey defined the rest of his life and all the theories he formed. Throughout his meticulously chronicled travels, later published as *The Voyage of the Beagle*, Darwin constantly sent back animal and plant specimens to Cambridge, where a good friend preserved them until his return. Consider the kind of deep imagination Darwin must have employed to make the leap from the on-site observations in his journals to his ultimate theory of natural selection. Like Milton's magnum opus, Darwin's life work as presented in *On the Origin of Species* is itself his own version of a theodicy, noting that the natural world is a continual life cycle of competition, suffering, and death.

In the concluding paragraphs of his work, however, Darwin reminds his readers that this cycle is the law impressed upon the world by the Creator, and that this has only led to the continual evolution of "endless forms most beautiful."

When I finally encountered Milton's Mulberry, alone in Cambridge in the summer of 2017, it was rather a sacramental experience. Having entered Christ's College through the great gate off St. Andrew's Street and nodded to the porter, I walked around the immaculate green lawn of the first court. The day was clear and warm, and I came upon no one else on my walk through the college grounds. I would need to pass through the campus' three courts on my way to the tree, but already I could almost feel it, like a pulsing presence.

My imagination was sparked. I had waited for this moment for a long while, and I reminded myself that Milton and Darwin, writer and scientist respectively, employed their imaginations to the maximum extent in their work. I followed the walkway through the second court, then the third, all the while flanked by tall stoic stone edifices. Everything was quiet and still on this lazy afternoon. Just ahead and to my left was the Darwin Garden, a botanical display of plants the naturalist would have encountered on his voyage, which I planned to visit afterward. To my right was an old dark brick wall, covered with clinging vines. Above the wall I could see the tops of the thick tree canopy on the other side, rising like an awning over a hallowed area.

In the brick wall was a green wooden door, swung outward toward the flora beyond. As I crossed the threshold, the air seemed to thicken alongside my anticipation. Turning left, I entered a tunnel of shadows made by the overhanging branches of the trees, the bright light of the sun delicately flickering through from above. As I walked deliberately along the arched pathway, the pulse of the tree became more pronounced, though I recognized it as my own heartbeat.

A moment later I was in the clearing, the mulberry before me at last. I spent some time sitting and reading in the grass under the tree, imagining all the thinkers of the past who may have enjoyed this very reading spot, this very shade. The person who walked out of that garden that day was not the same person who walked in. I imagined my visit as a kind of rebirth, a baptism by the cosmic universality of time and place. What strung together all these ideas in my mind was a desire for knowledge, and the continual pursuit of the elements that perpetually lay just beyond my reach.

Fleeing the plague in 1665, Milton moved his family to the English countryside. At his cottage home, Milton's daughters would help him complete *Paradise Lost.* Due to his blindness, and notwithstanding their difficult relationships with their father, they became his readers and his scribes. These days, the garden of Milton's cottage home has been planted with flowers from the Garden of Eden, as described in his epic poem. This sensuous passage is an example of Milton's esteem of life's abundancy, a vital component of the world, even amid the story of the Fall of Man. In essence, the idea that humanity comes to possess the knowledge of good and evil is the crux of Darwin's view at the end of *On the Origin of* Species. Death and suffering are validated as forces that eventually produce a moral being—in a word, us.

In 1842, Darwin and his family relocated to the rural Down House in 1842, where he lived out the rest of his life. It was here that he synthesized the ideas of his lifetime, making indispensable contributions to evolutionary science, botany, and geology. On the grounds of his house was a path, the sandwalk, where he could stroll and think under the towering trees astride it, some of which he'd planted himself. On a fitting note, Darwin had his own mulberry tree at Down House, under which he enjoyed watching his children play. One might think that, because his theories were entrenched with the brutality of the organism's survival and the tectonic shifts of deep time, Darwin would have a bleak disposition. As I write this story, during the summer of 2020, it is not difficult for the world to be shaded with a bleak view. Suffering and resolve have become focal points in my current reflections on our era of uncertainty.

Still, thoughts of Milton's Mulberry, and Darwin's botanical garden next to it, often float back to me. These gardens represent a point from which two apparently conflicting views of creation radiated out into the world. The more I think it about, though, the more these two views appear compatible and resonant with the same eternal mysteries. Reflecting on that singular afternoon soon thereafter, I understood the internal transformation that my pilgrimage to the tree signified.

Back home, halfway across the world, my family was waiting for my return. The embodiment of fatherhood had always been fully entwined in the notions of the birth of new life, and the incessant exploration of new knowledge. Awaiting my return with special eagerness were my young daughters: two forms of life most perfect and beautiful.

4

"The sage's heart is stilled! Heaven and Earth are reflected in it, the mirror of all life."

The Hunter & The Sage

When I was a child, my father taught me how to spot Orion in the night sky. We would often look up upon returning home from running some errand. As he would point out the constellation above, we would identify the star Betelgeuse. This red supergiant that makes up Orion's rear shoulder is one of the brightest in the heavens; yet it is hundreds of light years away. If Betelgeuse were to suddenly vanish, its absence would not be observable from earth for another 642 years. As I lay in my bed before falling asleep on those nights, I would contemplate the vast distances of the cosmos, as unfathomable to me as they were. In this way, I learned that even when fully entrenched in life's necessary mundanities, the mind can travel to places that are literally otherworldly.

The mythos of Orion the Hunter is complex and varied. One thread in the ancient Greek stories tells of how Zeus placed Orion in the heavens after his death by the sting of Scorpius, a punishment for The Hunter's rapacious desire to hunt down the animals of the earth. On clear nights, I have often noted the blue supergiant Rigel, the resplendent forward foot of The Hunter. In those moments, I imagine the countless individuals of past generations receding into deep time, those who have also looked up and wondered. I recall that one ancient world theory of the cosmos was that the night sky was a velvet dome, and each star a pin prick which teasingly revealed the magnificent blinding light beyond. My ruminations also bring to mind the medieval Buddhist monk Kenko, who wrote: "It is a most wonderful comfort to sit alone beneath a lamp, book spread before you, and commune with someone from the past whom you have never met."[1] With these words, Kenko refers to the writings of those before him, whose language extends across the eons. Similarly, the language of the night sky are the constellations, whose stories and lore reach through time and traverse civilizations.

Kenko's work is significant to me for its form and ideas. In his collected writings called *Tsurezuregusa*, or "Essays in Idleness," Kenko observed and recorded the world around himself with detail and wisdom. His observations of the natural world led to insight on how a human being should mindfully and meaningfully live. Aphoristic in form, his writings are like dewpoints of thought plucked from the world and placed within his personal vessel of knowledge, and we are grateful that it has survived the eons to be

---

[1] *Essays in Idleness*, p. 27

read and contemplated. His astute dictums are like flowers picked from a universal garden and placed in a vase for posterity. Consider the following: "I have relinquished all that ties me to the world, but the one thing that still haunts me is the beauty of the sky."[2] The import of Kenko's ascetic life and written recordings of nature was reiterated hundreds of years afterward in the work of Henry David Thoreau, who wrote: "Of what significance the light of day, if it is not the reflection of an inward dawn? -- to what purpose is the veil of night withdrawn, if the morning reveals nothing to the soul?"[3]

Revelatory Constellations

The age-old stories and myths of the constellations are revelatory to the soul, as they are wrought with the fabric of the human condition. According to the eminent mythologist Joseph Campbell, cultures and civilizations have projected their "deepest hopes, desires and fears, potentialities and conflicts" unto the night sky.[4] The stories of our ancestors' collective gods and goddesses were reflected in the firmament, and in fact served as a representation of the world around them. Consider the constellation Ursa Major, or the Great Bear. The mythology of the Great Bear stretches back to prehistoric times, both in European and Native American folklore. The bear symbolizes power, an animal to be respected and feared, but also one whose furs provide warmth and comfort. In some ancient European cultures, it is theorized, there was an intimate connection between bears and

---

[2] Ibid
[3] *Night and Moonlight,* p. 40
[4] *The Inner Reaches of Outer Space,* p. 55

humans. This includes the concept that the human race had previously been a race of bears, and that the upright gait of the bear confirms this. The Berserkers of the Old Norse sagas are said to have summoned the power of the bear and channeled it into an ecstatic state. This bear cult would wear the skin of a bear in battle, throwing violent fury to the wind and sky. Thus, wearing the bear-shirt induced one to go 'ber-serk;' the etymological connection is clear.[5] The Pima tribe of the American Southwest alludes to the divinity of the bear and sky in their "Bear Song," conjoining the language of the sky with the wildlife in their midst. They sing: "I am the Black Bear. Around me you see the clouds swirling."[6]

The Great Bear constellation has various names across cultures and eras. Some see a Big Dipper in the stars that make up the bear's hindquarters, a reminder of nourishment and the vitality of water. Ancient Chinese societies imagined a Celestial Palace; in medieval England it was Charles' Wain or the Plough. Some Christian sects in the Middle Ages recognized this constellation as the Heavenly Chariot. The Big Dipper moniker reminds one also of the Moon Rabbit of eastern cultures, where the lunar hare is mixing a bowl of stew or pounding rice cakes. The folklore of some Pacific island cultures, on the other hand, instead see a crab, with its claw reaching toward and around the topmost curvature of the moon. The constellation Scorpius is yet another example of how a particular civilization's myths and lore offer various symbology to the night sky. The scorpion, as I have mentioned, is in some stories a celestial companion to the punished Orion. In ancient China, on

---

[5] *The Ice-Shirt,* p. 371
[6] *Native American Songs and Poems,* p. 10

the other hand, Scorpius was recognized as a great dragon, gloriously rising above the horizon in the skies of summer.[7] These stories and myths, of course, constitute only a small fraction of the world mythology concerning the stars. Their telling and their analyses can be found in libraries long since written and preserved.

What is important to note is that these stories are ingrained into human history, a role that is somewhat lost to our current times, in the popular sense at least. Astrology has kept alive the traditions of the cosmos' influence on human fate. Astronomy continues to lay out the physics and science of the universe. Religions have internalized the symbols and divine meanings of the heavens. Art throughout history has represented the mystical and natural beauty of the skies. What I look for, however, is a personal communion with the stars: a connection without model, without name, and without limit. The stars, therefore, are the luminous guides on my path to gnosis. My pathwork lies within as well as on the astral plane; and yet they are one and the same. Essentially, this self-knowledge is the complete awareness of the psychological process and its obscurities.

Interstellar Architecture

The architecture of my inner experience has its foundation in the outer reaches. Our bodies, and all matter we know of that exists, are quite literally composed of stardust. The elements that comprise the organism were once embedded within the churning spheres of gas out there in the vast dark. Dying stars that have

---

[7] *The Soul of the Night,* p. 207

exploded in supernovae throughout the past billions of years fashioned the particles that make up our brains, our hearts, our skin. Nebulae stretching across light years once held the particles of our own creation. Looking up to the night sky, therefore, we look into the deep past of elemental creation. The capacity for thought has developed from an epoch of reproduction in the primordial soup to the contemplation of the cosmos in literature and art. To us, the duration of time seems incomprehensibly long, yet it is only a blink of astronomical time. At present, while some of us recognize only what we have come to know, some of us and thirst for that which has been occulted.

All in all, consciousness allows us to negotiate the physical world, to deliberate about our relationship to it, and to apprehend the numinous. Dr. Edgar Mitchell was an astronaut who founded the Institute of Noetic Sciences for the study of consciousness. He knew full well the mystical yet very real transformation that one can undergo at the contact point of awareness and the unknown. He is a witness to the immensity of space and within it the relative smallness and insignificance of our home planet. His epiphany in space kindled a new kind of understanding and fueled his latter-life drive towards studying the intimacies of the inner experience. What Mitchell experienced on his voyage between the moon and Earth is a documented phenomenon known as the Overview Effect, which "represents a fundamental transformation in cognition."[8] Seeing isolated Earth against the backdrop of the infinite chasm of space has resulted in numerous other astronauts reporting this very same kind of epiphany. In his book *The Way of*

---

[8] *The Cosma Hypothesis,* p. 123

the Explorer, Mitchell theorizes about the ways in which the cosmos are, to echo the words of Thoreau, revelatory to the soul: What if human consciousness is the universe's way of *knowing itself?*[9]

Bibliophilic Baptism

Long before I had encountered these heady ideas in any organized way, I lay my head upon my pillow and projected my youthful imagination. This is where I suppose my journey outward into the cosmos began. During those youthful days I spent considerable time concealed within the stacks of the small public library near my childhood home. The library was in actuality mere steps away, somewhat squat and unassuming between a few meager grocery and hardware stores. Hence, my baptism was by books. Clear are the memories I have of a midweek summer day when the library had just opened its doors, and I had the place all to myself. I became familiar with the kindly septuagenarian ladies who placidly carried out the library's daily operations. This sanctuary was unreachable to the bustle and commotion of the outside world. Slowly pacing up and down the aisles, I remember discovering topics and writers, stacking books up and sitting at table in the corner to handle them and appreciate them. As I gazed about the towering shelves, at least to my eyes at that stature, I felt at home. Looking back, it was actually a womblike comfort, but at the same time the desire for all the knowledge that lay before me was intensely sparked. I recall my imagination becoming overloaded with the discovery of tomes that became close to my heart, by writers such as Jules Verne, H.G. Wells, and Arthur C. Clarke.

---

[9] *The Way of the Explorer,* p. 234

This feeling has proven to be an insatiable desire that has never waned.

Now, my hearth is my home library, an alchemical lab of-letters. Ever since those early days alone in the library, my goal has been to resurrect the sublimity of being ensconced by physical books, sacred vessels of knowledge and feeling. As a hearth radiates warmth, so too does the roaring fire within each tome, so that collectively the conflagration burns bright. In his book *The Library at Night,* Alberto Manguel offers many ways in which the collection of books manifests itself. He declares that the library is at once myth, order, power, and a mirror of the mind. In his chapter "The Library as Workshop," he writes that, for readers, the home library is like "a den or a nest, holding the shape of their bodies and offering a container to their thoughts."[10]

As a book collector and student of the esoteric, a most vital aspect of my own pathwork has been the notebook. I proffer that this tool is absolutely essential to the seeker on any path. A journal in which to write, and one to always keep close, may take on many forms and purposes. Whether to record one's travels, dreams, or reading impressions, it is a method to negotiate inner experience. Every thinker I have admired, whether current or in the past, has kept notebooks. Their modeling was the reason I first started keeping my own notebooks, and their use has become a rather natural extension of my own mind.

The specific type of notebook that is relevant to this essay is a type that has been utilized for hundreds of years: the florilegium.

---

[10] *The Library at Night,* p. 178

In the middle ages, this was a collection of passages extracted from holy scripture or other learned writing. It was a tool of devotional study in the monastic life, one that recorded particularly relevant passages in the reading at hand. They were also used as teaching tools, to lecture or preach while expressing the exact words of the text under study. Unlike a journal of personal impressions or reviews, wherein a reader might respond to the text or analyze a concept, this type of notebook is more a set of observations, a reflection of a reader's consumed reading. In the florilegium, books are condensed into a collection of quotes, so that the points of text where new ideas had spontaneously bloomed are preserved. It serves as "an act of homage and submission to a text that has begun to speak to us but which we would love to penetrate more."[11]

As I work, my florilegia become vessels in which the language of my guides has been assembled. Imagine the home library as a garden, and as one walks through its paths, passages are plucked and placed in a vase to be saved and kept fresh. When I need to refer to these passages, I can go back and find them gathered together, a contemplation technique actually discussed by Kenko. The word 'florilegium' itself comes from the Latin words *flos* and *legere,* which literally denote the gathering of flowers. Other florilegia, some that date back to the middle ages as well, are not reading notebooks, but actually botanical treatises.

Some of these were texts on herbal medicine and others were collections of floral artwork. Gathering words, then, turns out to be as natural as gathering flowers.

---

[11] *Sacred Reading,* p. 84

Near the end of his book, Alberto Manguel presents the concept of the library as home. I identify with his suggestion, as should all students of the esoteric, for it is the haven inside which The Great Work germinates. However, in order to expand knowledge, we must necessarily venture outside the laboratory to heed the call of that which summons from near or afar. In the summer of 2017, I heard and answered the call of Stonehenge. Along with my family, I packed my bags, brought along an empty suitcase for newly collected book acquisitions, and soon found myself across the Atlantic Ocean and amidst the Salisbury Plain of south-central England. My lifelong interest in astronomy, as well as my work in the mystery tradition, compelled me towards the ancient stone monument. What attracted me is the sacred quality of the ruins, and its connection to the obscure history of the remote past. In essence, I sought to bypass the scripts of history proper and directly confront the numinous. It was a pilgrimage to a place that had always seized my cosmic imagination, yet existed upon the physical earth.

Megalithic Soul

Emerging out of prehistoric belief systems, Stonehenge was erected as a monument to the summer and winter solstices. During elder times, the cathedral's celestial dome was emblematic of humanity's primeval temple. Long before the traditions of institutionalized religions, mankind used the stars to navigate everyday life. Across the globe, as is illustrated in astronomer Chet Raymo's book *The Soul of the Night,* virtually all known early societies worshiped the skies. We, too, can strip away the calendric weight of the modern mundane world and look to the same constellations, planets, and comets that those early humans did long ago. My experience at Stonehenge was like stepping through a gateway, wherein one way of thinking had ended and another way begun. This idea was in fact rooted in the most natural beauty.

Upon arriving at the Stonehenge plain, I was immediately struck by an unexpected visual: the array of rich red poppies growing throughout the field. At that moment, I realized that a new kind of florilegium had come into my mind. As a matter of fact, I did have my notebooks in my backpack in that moment. With my new florilegium, however, I would record my observations of the otherworldly. Raymo's own words are apt for my frame of mind as I deliberately walked widdershins around the ancient megaliths: "we must enter into the universe of the galaxies and the light-years, *even at the risk of spiritual vertigo,* and know after all what must be known."[12]

Exactly how to access the unknown is an eternal question. Here I recall the exhortation of Antonius Block, the medieval knight in Ingmar Bergman's film *The Seventh Seal.* He says, "I want knowledge. Not faith, not suppositions, but knowledge."[13] He pronounces his raw desire for that which is occulted to the figure of Death himself, who of course has no intention of divulging his secrets. The abrupt insight I experienced at Stonehenge on that blustery afternoon was something akin to the revelation of what is called cosmic consciousness. This state could be described as the concept of the unity of all things, however ephemerally recognized.

---

[12] *The Soul of the Night,* p. ix
[13] *Four Screenplays of Ingmar Bergman,* p. 112

It is open to anyone with a sensitivity for modes of perception beyond language and an imaginative spirit to support a journey into the unknown.

The human nervous system's capacity to enter and negotiate altered states of consciousness is known to psychology. Skeptics often misinterpret this event as some type of exaggerated performance.

However, the simple act of reading a book or listening to music foments a change of consciousness. Modern physics has been moving towards the theory of cosmic consciousness for centuries, with the last several decades boasting breakthroughs in the models of universal energy and particle physics.

The celebrated astronomer Carl Sagan argued that stars are absolutely alive with the same energies that comprise the human being. As nebulae coalesced into colossal blazing furnaces of gas that would become the inaugural stars, he proposed, "the ash of stellar alchemy was now emerging into consciousness."[14] William James, in his classic text *The Varieties of Religious Experience,* details the state of cosmic consciousness, in which individuals confront the energy of the universe directly, bypassing the mind-body construct entirely.

He warns that this mystical state should not be viewed as some vague and sentimental experience, for his research showed this is as authentic and valid as any state of spiritual apprehension.

---

[14] *Cosmos,* p. 360

Furthermore, James analyzes the work of Richard Maurice Bucke, who chronicled the experiences of cosmic consciousness throughout history, religion, science, and literature. These include passages and experiences from a wide range of cultures and eras.

The cathartic account of Guatama the Buddha is represented, as is a narrative in the Book of Exodus. Seminal geologist Charles Lyell recorded his own ecstatic episode of cosmic consciousness, as did others such as William Blake and Charles Darwin in their books. [15]

Numerous ancient traditions believed in the interconnectedness of the natural elements, from the heavenly bodies to the organs of the human body, far prior to the modern religious milieu. The Mayans understood human existence as a living reflection of cosmic consciousness. [16] Eastern mysticism especially has espoused the idea that the universe is a single unit sharing an awareness across space. Exactly how this awareness manifests itself in the individual is realized through a rigorous journey of self-knowledge.

The descriptions of these events all share similar aspects of language and interpretation. They reveal sudden knowledge of a close and inexorable connection with the universe-- indeed, a knowledge of being a participant in it. This is gnosis that is best expressed through what Joseph Campbell calls "the way of art": music, visuals, and poetic language. Walt Whitman's poetic works, which were also studied by Bucke, are replete with revelations of

---

[15] *Cosmic Consciousness*, p. 191
[16] *Secrets of Mayan Science/Religion*, p. 25

infinite mind. In his poem "When I Heard the Learn'd Astronomer," the narrator walks out of a stuffy astronomy lesson and into the "mystical moist night-air," where he, "from time to time, Look'd up in perfect silence at the stars."[17] Reflecting on the reorganization of mind I sensed at Stonehenge, I recapitulated to myself the query of astronaut Edgar Mitchell: What if human consciousness is the universe's way of *knowing itself?* I knew then that my work would be to look up and observe outward in order to more deeply journey inward. To negotiate the night sky, therefore, is to negotiate the spirit of flesh and blood. Harking back to the ancients who crafted stories out of the constellations, I imagined a reset button hit in my cognition, wherein the structure of prior knowledge was turned blank. Further, I imagined that the sacred stone ruins of Stonehenge had resonated with a provocation to not only be an *observer*, but a *participant* in the cosmic machinations. It was the initiation of the florilegium stellarum.

The Star-Gaze

In her book *The Human Cosmos,* Jo Marchant posits that the disconnect between the spiritual lives of humans and outer space is largely due to the simple fact that the stars and planets cannot be seen as clearly as they once could. Throughout the past few centuries, global industrialization has rendered the atmosphere obscure with pollutants. Not only are chemical pollutants to blame, but also the light pollution of urban landscapes. The stars and planets are literally occult. In my own city setting, an

---

[17] *Leaves of Grass,* p. 219

observation of the night sky relies on the convergence of clear weather and an effort to consult the star maps.

As I look upwards on those occasional crystalline evenings, it is easy to be overtaken by a sense of the sublime. The sheer reality of deep space and infinity is available to anyone willing to see.

One can imagine turning the pages of the most immense and antiquarian book, for the search for occult knowledge requires a receptive and exploratory state of mind. The observations made on these nights are recorded in the florilegium stellarum, my notebook of the stars. In doing so, the conversation with the self is sustained; for if consciousness is the universe's way of knowing itself, then we must gaze outward in order to more deeply journey inward.

It is noteworthy that virtually all the instances of cosmic consciousness related throughout history take place outdoors in a natural setting. This reminds one of the essentiality of going into nature as a respite from the everyday minutia that builds up over time to clog the psyche. As a backyard stargazer, I can attest to the cleansing nature of the majestic night sky. In this instance, I am not only an observer but a participant.

When observing and recording, as the physicist Werner Heisenberg said, one "does not simply describe and explain nature; it is part of the interplay between nature and ourselves."[18] The florilegium stellarum, then, takes on meaning that is both personal and universal. Early humans built megalithic monuments to venerate the sun, the moon, and stars. Cosmological rituals were undoubtedly held at Stonehenge, acknowledged by scholars due to

---

[18] *The Tao of Physics*, p. 140

the discovery of sophisticated alignments of its structure to calculated astronomical events, especially the midwinter and midsummer solstices.[19] Since I of course have no means to replicate their efforts, my veneration is channeled into stargazing.

This process is ritualized by setting up gear, locating my astral destination, and meditatively writing my observations.

In Kim Stanley Robinson's novel *Shaman,* the spiritual leader of a band of early humans uses a tally stick to mark the passage of time. During an ice age, before the provenance of written language, he carefully observes the phases of the moon. As each cycle comes and goes, he makes another notch in the stick. Eventually, his observational work leads to knowledge of seasonal changes and the solstices. There is some archaeological evidence that early humans may have used similar tally sticks, not only to measure out the months but to record star patterns-- could these be signs of the first recorded constellations? Judging from some examples of organized notches in animal bones, there may have been individuals since the dawn of mankind who shared the same wonder as I currently experience in my back yard, binoculars and notebook in hand. Campbell writes of the *mysterium tremendum et fascinans,* a feeling which corresponds to the "everlasting fire which is exploding in the galaxies, blazing in the sun, reflected in the moon, and coursing as the ache of desire through our veins."[20] Moreover, there is evidence that primeval stargazers may have transformed their wonder into shamanic journeys which culminated in cave paintings that depict

---

[19] *Prehistoric Astronomy and Ritual,* p. 9
[20] *The Inner Reaches of Outer Space,* p. 135

constellations.[21] Thusly did these ice age shamans astrally project themselves outward, perhaps with support of herbal substances, in order to venture inward and down into the underground caves: the womb of Mother Earth.

The walls of these caves may have acted as the blank pages upon which they recorded their own devotional celestial observations.

One of the most distinctive features of the night sky, whose representation has been traced back deep into prehistory, is The Pleiades star cluster. Like other prominent points on the star maps, they played a vital role in much of the history around the globe, from sea navigation to the development of the telescope. For me, the sense of awe at recognizing The Pleiades in the night sky never fades. When I encounter them with the naked eye, which is not altogether common in my metropolitan home setting, they are a hazy patch near Aldebaran, the red eye of Taurus the bull. With an unfaltering gaze, however, they begin to materialize out of the velvet dark. The Seven Sisters, as they are also known, are named for Atlas's daughters of Greek mythology; a nearby star is named for the father himself.[22]

The notches made on that ice age bone are conceivably the stars of the Seven Sisters. Eons hence, on a clear cold December night, I make my own entry into the florilegium stellarum. If it is particularly clear, I shift my searching gaze to Orion's Sword, the center of which is the Orion Nebula, over one thousand light years

---

[21] *The Human Cosmos,* 17
[22] *Star Names: Their Lore and Meaning,* p. 391

away and twenty-four light years across. Looking at this mere speck of misty light through my telescopic lenses, I am no less awed by the majestic cloud of interstellar gas.

In *Paradise Lost,* John Milton wrote of "this Earth, a spot, a grain, an atom, with the firmament compared and all her numbered stars, that seem to roll spaces incomprehensible."[23] Indeed, I stand here on this Earth, where I will live out the days of my life, and from time to time, look up in perfect silence at the stars. Those points of light are worlds unto themselves, seemingly affixed out in space incomprehensible. The Orion Nebula is a vast diffusion of stardust where matter is born, and wherefrom the elemental ingredients that make up human life comes. Could it be that I know, somewhere within the inner reaches of my consciousness, that as I lift my gaze to the starry heavens, I look towards home?

Bibliography

Allen, Richard Hinkley. *Star Names: Their Lore and Meaning.* Dover, 1963.

Bucke, Maurice Andrews. *Cosmic Consciousness,* edited by G.M. Acklom. Arkana, 1991.

Burl, Aubrey. *Prehistoric Astronomy and Ritual.* Shire, 1983.

Campbell, Joseph. *The Inner Reaches of Outer Space.* Harper Perennial, 1986.

Capra, Fritjof. *The Tao of Physics.* Shambhala, 2000.

Casey, Michael. *Sacred Reading.* Harper Collins, 1995.

James, William. *The Varieties of Religious Experience.* Collier, 1961.

---

[23] *Paradise Lost,* p. 181

Malmstrom, Lars and David Kushner, eds. *Four Screenplays of Ingmar Bergman.* Simon and Schuster, 1960.

Manguel, Alberto. *The Library at Night.* Yale, 2006.

Marchant, Jo. *The Human Cosmos.* Dutton, 2020.

Milton, John. *Paradise Lost,* edited by Scott Elledge. Norton, 1993.

Mitchell, Edgar. *The Way of the Explorer.* New Page, 2008.

McKinney, Meredith, translator. *Kenko and Chomei: Essays in Idleness and Hojoki.* Penguin, 2013.

Men, Hunbatz. *Secrets of Mayan Science/Religion.* Bear & Company, 1990.

Palmer, Martin, translator. *The Book of Chuang Tzu.* Penguin, 2006.

Pearson, Mike Parker. *Stonehenge: A New Understanding.* The Experiment, 2011.

Raymo, Chet. *The Soul of the Night.* Crowley, 1992.

Robinson, Kim Stanley. *Shaman.* Orbit, 2013.

Sagan, Carl. *Cosmos.* Ballantine, 1980.

Swann, Brian, editor. *Native American Songs and Poems.* Dover, 1996.

Thoreau, Henry David. *Night and Moonlight,* edited by Read & Co. Read & Co., 2020.

Vollmann, William T. *The Ice-Shirt.* Penguin, 1990.

White, Frank. *The Cosma Hypothesis.* Morgan Brook, 2019.

Whitman, Walt. *Leaves of Grass,* edited by Justin Kaplan. Bantam, 1983.

5

The Path of the Labyrinth

In April 2020, during the darkest days of the global pandemic, a community gathered to play hopscotch. Over 1,300 squares of the game were drawn onto the sidewalk of Leamington Terrace in Edinburgh, eventually reaching 400 meters in length. Children and adults alike took up chalk, squatted down to the pavement, and added to the neighborhood project. It eventually became emblematic of connectedness and empathy as the virus raged on. In a world quickly becoming difficult to recognize amid fear and confusion, this children's game acted as a symbol of assurance and orientation.

The ladder design of the hopscotch court evokes a ceremonial pathway, a personal challenge to reach the end goal. In times past, this goal was called heaven, or sometimes hell. Hopscotch is likely an extant remnant of ancient rituals, many whose precise functions are now forgotten. Folk memory, however, has preserved some of the ancient patterns and symbols in the shadows of history and culture.

The labyrinth is one such pattern, whose ubiquity reveals a deep affinity with myth and folklore. Like a hopscotch court unraveled, the labyrinth is a unicursal figure that has been used not only to search for meaning and endurance, but also as a source of magical protection and mystical guidance. A true labyrinth follows a single path to the center and back out again, without choices nor obstacles besides endurance and concentration.

Some of the earliest symbols associated with the labyrinth are the Neolithic cup-and-ring petroglyphs such as those found along coastal Scotland. Spiral designs from the same era are cut into stone at Newgrange, Ireland, the type of rock carvings found all along the Atlantic coastline. This geographical stretch, from Scandinavia southward through the British Isles and the Iberian Peninsula, showcases carvings with the spiral patterns found in nature that must have fascinated prehistoric humankind.

Echoes of magic and myth

Among the early petroglyphs are those that hint at the labyrinth as magical tool. Along the Galician coastline of present-day Spain occur several true labyrinths of prehistoric origin. On one rock outcrop is a carving of figures on horseback chasing a herd of deer, while yet another is a vignette with five labyrinths and several antlered deer. Could the Galician labyrinths have been some form of hunting magic, as some researchers suggest? Conceivably they symbolized a trap for prey, or a warning to avoid treacherous ground.

There is some basis for hunting magic's connection to the labyrinth in the Icelandic myth of Wayland's House, in which a hero is tasked to hunt down and kill a monster within a labyrinth. In the tale, the *honocentaurus* is lured into the center of a twisting, winding structure with a chunk of honeyed boar meat and ultimately slain.

This story is a retelling of the classical myth of the Minotaur, the creature in the labyrinth who Theseus vanquishes with the help of Ariadne. She secretly assists Theseus with a ball of thread, which he uses to navigate the intricate structure and confront the Minotaur, who possesses the body of a man and the head of a bull. The name of Daedalus, the architect of the Cretan labyrinth, lived on throughout the Middle Ages, for labyrinths were often called Houses of Daedalus.

On the island of Delos, Theseus later performs a dance that reenacts his journey through the labyrinth. The performance imitated the winding circuitry of the Daedalian passageways. Scholars suggest that this dance also mimics celestial harmony, in which the seven planets (known at the time) trace the sky in spherical motion. This connection is made stronger when recognizing that the classical labyrinth form, dating back to prehistoric rock carvings, indeed contain seven circuits. These archetypal performances are some of the foundations of collective human ritual.

An amalgamation of the seven symbolic circuits is represented by a 17th century illustration by the German polymath Athanasius Kircher (1602-1680). In it, the god Pan stands with his left hand outstretched and encircled by cosmic rings, while within each ring is each planet's sigil. His flute is aligned with the circular pattern so that the seven notes of the musical scale are in harmony, while the celestial spheres mimic the outlines of the seven-colored rainbow. Embodied in Pan is the human-animal hybridity that recalls the Minotaur.

Labyrinths have for ages been abodes of the mythical. Pliny (23-79 CE) describes the great Egyptian labyrinth of the ancient world as thronged with statues of gods, kings, and monsters. Herodotus (484-425 BCE) writes of its perilous lower chambers entombed with dead kings and sacred crocodiles. Historians of antiquity marveled at its complex construction and astounding magnitude. Archeologist Sir Arthur Evans' unearthing of a palace at Knossos in Crete, fully excavated in 1905, sparked speculation of bull cults that pumped life into the myth of the Cretan labyrinth. Early Knossos coins were emblazoned with the labyrinth symbol, carrying the myth further through the ages.

Another artifact that hints at prehistoric rites is a wine jug found in an Etruscan tomb. Its design displays an equestrian event, with horseback riders trotting out of a labyrinth. In *The Aeneid,* the poet Virgil (70-19 BCE) records a theatrical ritual performed at funerals, a processional called the *Ludus Trojae* or Game of Troy. Curiously, the labyrinth on the jug is labeled as Troy, a fallen city that seemed invincible but ultimately proved vulnerable. Labyrinths, especially those meant for walking, were in subsequent centuries often named after the city of Troy. An exemplar is the "Walls of Troy," a 19th century labyrinth at Rockcliffe, on the shores of Scotland's Solway Firth.

Divine Designs

Pioneering researcher W.H. Matthews suggests that prehistoric rites are broadly connected and widely spread expressions. These ceremonials, he writes, may have been "associated with the awakening of nature in spring, [. . .] the release of the imprisoned sun after its long captivity in the toils of the demon of winter."

The earliest labyrinth designs associated with Christianity are often found in ruins, such as Ireland's Hollywood Stone. These normally date to before 1000 CE. Around that time, the medieval labyrinth also appeared in illustrated manuscripts that circulated throughout monasteries and cathedral libraries. They sometimes featured prayers within their passageways, or devilish figures in their centers. Theseus and the Minotaur appear at the center of various labyrinths in medieval manuscripts, demonstrating the enduring strength and acceptance of the myth. The pagan symbol of the labyrinth eventually became a central mystical symbol of several medieval Christian churches, with an especial significance at Easter.

The medieval labyrinth can best be identified by its eleven-circuit pattern, yet with still only one unobstructed track. They soon made the transition from manuscript to Church pavement. As one scholar notes, "the unicursal wanderer must submit completely" to its course, a concept that engrossed the medieval Christian mind. The best-known example is the Chartres Cathedral labyrinth, laid around 1202. Throughout the Middle Ages, pilgrims visited in hope of tracing its sacred geometry and to experience the divine. The mystical purgation-illumination-union ritual of walking to the center was equated to Christ's Harrowing of Hell, in turn mythologically associated with the quest of Theseus.

A beguiling ritual was first recorded in 1396 at Auxerre Cathedral. As an Easter Sunday celebration, the clergy gathered on the pavement labyrinth to play a game called *pilota,* in which a large leather ball was tossed from cleric to cleric. They joined hands, chanted, and performed a snake dance. There are theories that this symbolic ceremony was connected to ancient folk traditions associated with sun worship, perhaps reimagined within Christianity as the *Sol Resurrectionis.*

The Lore of Turf And Stone

Traces of various folkloric dances are common wherever labyrinths are found. The Maiden's Bower was a game in which a girl stood at the center while boys rushed along the winding path to reach her. These outdoor games were played on the turf labyrinths that mostly originated in the late Middle Ages and continued through the Renaissance. At least thirty turf labyrinths are recorded in Britain as having been grown and cultivated on village greens for local fairs, of which only a few survive to this day. Records show that they were often a feature of May Day festivals. In an era of rampant disease and harsh conditions, these labyrinths were the hearts of much-needed kinship.

Eventually, outdoor pleasure gardens for the wealthy and aristocratic began to feature turf labyrinths and hedge mazes. These partly developed from the fabled Bower of Fair Rosamond, lover of Henry II. Sequestered and hidden from Queen Eleanor of Aquitaine inside a labyrinthine structure, Rosamond was eventually discovered, and in one version of the tale forced by Eleanor to imbibe a bowl of poison.

Labyrinths created in isolated landscapes were often regarded as liminal spaces, where walking its shape conjured pathways to the spirit world. A custom prevalent among Welsh shepherds was a design cut into the turf called the *caerdroia*. These may have developed out of deep past traditions, when the labyrinth was a protective binding magic against wolves. There are Scandinavian tales of fishermen using labyrinths to entrap the wind, thus creating more favorable weather on the water. Others tell of sea-gremlins lured into the stone labyrinths that dot the coastlines, ensnared so as to not follow the men onto their boats. The surviving stone labyrinth on the Isle of St. Agnes, off the tip of Cornwall, is a prehistoric example of these influences.

The Museum of Witchcraft and Magic in Boscastle has in its collections a ritual object called a Troy Stone, which was handed down through many generations of wise women. Engraved with a labyrinth, which would be followed with a finger, it was used for accessing altered states of consciousness. Thus, tracing the labyrinth's pattern induces an apprehension of the numinous. This idea is found in some magical practices across cultures. In Tantric India, for instance, there are accounts of midwives using the labyrinth design to assist in childbirth, believing that a mother's mental circumambulation of its path during labor would result in a safe delivery.

Well into the 19th century, some local festivals were celebrated by walking a turf labyrinth. Julian's Bower in North Lincolnshire was one such site, where in 1866 a witness reported seeing villagers at play while "under an indefinite persuasion of something unseen and unknown co-operating with them." Still in existence, Julian's Bower, near the river Trent, is also the home of a mischievous spirit. To frighten visiting pilgrims, the folk tale goes, the river spirit periodically compels waves to crash upon the land in attempt to wash away visitors.

An early medieval North Yorkshire castle once boasted a turf labyrinth, yet all that remains is a worn hollow atop a mound. Into the early 20th century, locals who walked it claimed to hear fairies singing in its center. Known as Fairy Hill, its design was probably influenced by Shepherd's Race labyrinth in Northamptonshire. Its treading was a tradition of a three-day feast of St. John celebration, which coincides with the summer solstice, and dates back to the 14th century. Legend has it that attempting to traverse the labyrinth three times would result in certain death, while an adjacent holy well augments the mystery of its obscure lore.

Among the labyrinth's multitudinous turns, the stages of life are analogously reflected. The vicissitudes of the human condition, from prehistoric times to the present, are represented in its singular pathway. Its recent revival as a mental health support and spiritual tool continues its profound healing effects. Like the hopscotch court in Edinburgh, labyrinths have been ritualistic sites of solidarity. Modern literature and cinema have further imbued popular consciousness with its universal imprint.

A 1981 exhibit at the Museo della Permanente in Milan featured a labyrinth which visitors were invited to enter. At its center they discovered a mirror closet, where they encountered an endless self-reflection. Perhaps the monsters in the labyrinth have always been ourselves. Still, to walk the path back out is to be reborn—and transformed from that which had walked in.

Sources

Bandiera, Nancy Ann. "The Medieval Labyrinth Ritual and Performance." 2006. The University of Texas at Austin, PhD dissertation.

Berk, Ari. "The Dance of the Labyrinth." *The Journal of Mythic Arts,* 2004, https://endicottstudio.typepad.com/articleslist/the-dance-of-the-labyrinth-by-ari-berk.html

Doob, Penelope Reed. *The Idea of the Labyrinth from Classical Antiquity Through the Middle Ages.* Cornell, 1990.

Jaskolski, Helmut. *The Labyrinth: Symbol of Fear, Rebirth, and Liberation.* Shambhala, 1997.

Kern, Hermann. *Through the Labyrinth: Designs and Meanings Over 5,000 Years.* Prestel, 2000.

Matthews, W.H. *Mazes & Labyrinths: Their Development and History.* Dover, 1970.

McKenzie, Jamie. "Giant hopscotch game with nearly 1,400 squares reaches end of 400m long Edinburgh street after several days of sunshine." *Edinburgh Evening News.* 25 April 2020, https://www.edinburghnews.scotsman.com/news/people/giant-hopscotch-game-nearly-1400-squares-reaches-end-400m-long-edinburgh-street-after-several-days-sunshine-2549482.

Pennick, Nigel. *Mazes and Labyrinths.* Robert Hale, 1990.

Saward, Jeff. *Labyrinths & Mazes: A Complete Guide to the Magical Paths of the World.* Lark, 2003.

6

And Yet it Deviated

Let us begin by putting ourselves in the proper state of mind. We exist in a vast universe. The great Carl Sagan once said that our planet is merely "a mote of dust suspended in a sunbeam." That is a poetic way of putting it, but using a scale model is just as astounding. If our sun were a grain of sand, for example, the nearest grain of sand would be four miles away. There are billions of grains in our galaxy alone, stars so far apart from each other that light takes thousands of years to travel between them. Now consider that there are over 100 billion observable galaxies, each with billions of stars like grains of sand spread across incomprehensible gulfs. Recent studies estimate that there are probably trillions of galaxies, adding to the definitive assurance of our astronomically miniscule existence.

In July of 2022, the NASA James Webb telescope released its first spectacular images of deep space. Reactions of wonder have abounded in the spheres of popular media, with many mesmerized by infrared shots of elegant swirling galaxies and majestic cosmic dust.

The high-tech precision and sharp vibrancy of the Webb pictures have ignited awe in deep space enthusiasts and casual news-readers alike. An article in *The Wall Street Journal* asserts that the Webb telescope "signals the start of a new era of space-borne astronomical observation." The article goes on to explain how robotic technologies continue to improve human understanding of the universe in ways that astronauts cannot.

Machines, therefore, are the future of exploration. They will serve as extensions of the human mind-body construct. Since they are able to capture light that the limited perceptions of the naked eye cannot perceive, the reliance on mechanized receptors will continue to develop. It is only natural that space exploration be the realm of machines. As Eric G. Wilson states in his book *The Melancholy Android*: "We require our computers to survive; they are extensions of our consciousness." This 21st century reality, he argues, has significantly augmented the subconscious anxieties of our time. The stunning images of deep space at once remind us of our frail aloneness as well as the persistent progress of technological communion. Wilson observes that the "ubiquitous blurring between human and machine has produced unprecedented emotional and epistemological confusions."

Along with the knowledge of the universe's size, it is important to keep in mind that the images from the Webb telescope are over 13 billion years old. This perspective brings to mind the potential for nonhuman intelligent life in the vast cosmos, and especially one particular aspect of the Fermi Paradox. The basic question of the paradox is, if aliens are out there, where are they? One of the possible solutions to this question is that alien civilizations may have long since developed and collapsed, considering the immense duration of time involved. According to a 2021 Space.com article, one view is that "the odds that we overlap in time and space with a detectable alien civilization don't seem great."

Recent data from the Hubble and Kepler space telescopes suggest that Earth is actually an early bloomer, relatively speaking. So, it is possible that not enough time has passed for intelligent life on other planets to have evolved enough to produce sufficiently advanced detectable technology. Even so, the current NASA Exoplanet Archive report lists a total of over 5,000 known exoplancts, many of which are in the habitable zone, a region that astrobiologists maintain could potentially breed life. NASA estimates that about half of all observable solar systems contain at least one planet in the habitable zone.

Space telescopes are the extension of humanity's eyes, while machines such as the six Mars rovers play the role of humanity's physical extremities. However, to actually travel beyond the solar system and into deeper space will require the types of innovation that physicist Michio Kaku discusses in his book *The Future of Humanity*. Specifically, he writes, "nanotechnology and artificial intelligence may drastically change the rules of the game" when it comes to developing a presence in outer space. In 2016, Stephen Hawking and Yuri Milner announced the Breakthrough Starshot Initiative, a project which endeavors to "develop 'nanoships,' sophisticated chips placed on sails energized by a huge bank of powerful laser beams on Earth." The mission is that by the year 2050, the diminutive machines would be launched from Earth towards a flyby of the Alpha Centauri star system 4.37 light years away, a destination to which it would take 20 years to arrive. The extant distances of the cosmos boggle the mind but also ignite the imagination. What if prospective alien civilizations are indeed out there, and have traversed a similar path of technological advancement as our own? Keeping in line with that path of logic, what if they have not visited us, but their small-scale machines have? It is unlikely that we would even notice their presence. In the same way that some of our own future technology is unimaginable in the present, it is probable that some of their technology would be unimaginable to us. Whether their space travel machines would be nanotechnology, or the flying saucers and spaceships that endure in the popular imagination, it would be a historic event to prove their existence. According to one leading astrophysicist, there actually does exist evidence of extraterrestrial technology.

"And yet it deviated." This is the key four-word sentence in astrophysicist Avi Loeb's book *Extraterrestrial: The First Sign of Intelligent Life Beyond Earth.* The book, published in 2021, argues that an object that passed through our solar system in 2017 was in actuality the first observation of intelligent alien design. Although dismissed as a highly unusual asteroid by some observers, Loeb, the long-serving chair of the astronomy department at Harvard University, strongly disagrees with that theory. The object entered the solar system, sped around the sun within the ellipse of Mercury, and continued its journey outward. Observed for several days by astronomers, the body of data shows that the object did not at all behave as expected.

This is true despite the fact that "universal laws of physics allow us to predict with certainty what a given object's trajectory should be." And yet it deviated. The Spitzer Space Telescope, which makes highly detailed celestial observations, did not detect the usual gas and heat that should have been emitted by the object. In addition to its thin cigar shape being an extreme figure in comparison to usual space objects, its physical composition proved challenging to validate. Interestingly, the object was at first classified as a comet, then reclassified as an asteroid. Finally, however, because of its ambiguity, a new designation had to be created, one that was neither comet nor asteroid: interstellar object. This is because the object is not bound to our sun's gravity, but rather comes from deep space.

The object's suggested original name was Rama, after the extraterrestrial spaceship in Arthur C. Clarke's science fiction novel *Rendezvous with Rama*. Nevertheless, since it was discovered by a Hawaiian observatory, it was named 'Oumuamua in the native Hawaiian language, which translates to *first distant messenger*. Clearly, the object's name, along with the puzzling aspects of its observation, are evocative of the alien machine prospect. The astronomers who observed the object for 30 hours and analyzed the data concluded their report's abstract with the following statement: "Our results extend the mystery of 'Oumuamua's origins and evolution."

The layered anomalous characteristics of 'Oumuamua, according to Loeb, would classify it as a one-in-a-million object, a figure mathematically drawn from the historical catalog of space objects. In his assessment, the data and analysis "clearly defy the understandable." In an interview with Space Explored, Loeb declares that "some people do not want to discuss the possibility that there are other civilizations out there. They believe we are special and unique. I think it's a prejudice that should be abandoned." In his book, he discusses at length his view that the traditional stigma surrounding extraterrestrial inquiry is bizarre, and that his academic field's general closed-mindedness is frustrating and unfortunate.

This skeptical mindset of much of academia notwithstanding, the stigma surrounding the topic of extraterrestrial study has diminished in recent years. A significant initiative called The Dr. Edgar Mitchell Foundation for Research into Extraterrestrial and Extraordinary Experiences, named after the NASA astronaut who took part in the project, conducted a rigorous scientific investigation that culminated in a 2018 publication called *Beyond UFOs*. This hefty report thoroughly collects contact experiences and witness testimony, along with academic articles from esteemed physicists, psychologists, and more. Its treatment of the nonhuman intelligence experience phenomenon is methodical and objective. Rudy Schild, astronomer at the Harvard-Smithsonian Center for Astrophysics, writes in the report that "We live in an exciting world where advances in space exploration and astrophysics are matched by the wonder of UAP sightings."

A 2021 article in *The New Yorker* titled "How the Pentagon Started Taking U.F.O.s Seriously" chronicles the recent history of unidentified aerial phenomena, from the famous 1947 Roswell incident through the U.S.S. Nimitz encounter of 2004 off the coast of California. Audiovisual documentation of the latter was released to the public by the Pentagon in 2020, and appears to show technology far beyond that of human capability. In the 2020 documentary film *The Phenomenon,* Commander David Fravor, one of the first of forty aviators who witnessed the astonishing abilities of the unknown vehicles during the Nimitz encounter, narrates his experience. He recognizes that it is highly unlikely that the objects he saw are of human origin. Commander Fravor's detailed description of his encounter is one of several recent examples of similar accounts by U.S. military personnel. In the film, Christopher Mellon, former U.S. Deputy Assistant Secretary of Defense, states that the main idea the public should know about unidentified aerial phenomena is that "these things are real, they're here, this is happening now."

Like the interstellar object 'Oumuamua, the strange vehicles recently witnessed by so many dependable sources, deviated from what is possible with current human technology. The extraterrestrial life debate goes back to antiquity, as is revealed by the written texts of philosophers, theologians, and astronomers throughout history. Michael J. Crowe, historian of extraterrestrial studies, believes that a contact with nonhuman intelligence is quite conceivably imminent. He wrote in the 1990s that "the detection of an extraterrestrial civilization" would certainly be "one of the most important discoveries that scientists ever sought."

Avi Loeb is certainly convinced that we already have undeniable evidence, and more and more people seem to be opening their minds to that possibility in the wake of mounting signs that are increasingly difficult to ignore. Human technological capacity for observation and documentation is rapidly growing as an extension of our perception, from the ubiquity of sophisticated cell phone cameras to the advanced new space telescopes. If alien technologies are indeed here, it will be progressively harder for them to elude observation. It may very well be that we are now on the cusp of otherworldly discovery, of real revelation.

Bibliography

Crowe, Michael J. *The Extraterrestrial Life Debate, 1750-1900.* Dover, 1999.

Loeb, Avi. *Extraterrestrial: The First Sign of Intelligent Life in the Universe.* Houghton Mifflin Harcourt, 2021.

"Harvard Science Professor Believes Interstellar Object Oumuamua Was Alien Tech, Not Rogue Comet." *Space Explored,* 4 January 2021, https://spaceexplored.com/2021/01/04/harvard-science-professor-believes-interstellar-object-oumuamua-was-alien-technology-not-a-rogue-comet/.

Hernandez, Rey, John Klimo and Rudy Schild, editors. *Beyond UFOs.* Free, 2018.

Howell, Elizabeth. "Fermi Paradox: Where are the aliens?" *Space.com,* 17 December 2021, https://www.space.com/25325-fermi-paradox.html.

Kaku, Michio. *The Future of Humanity.* Anchor Books, 2018.

Lewis-Kraus, Gideon. "How the Pentagon Started Taking U.F.O.s Seriously." *The New Yorker,* 30 April 2022, https://www.newyorker.com/magazine/2021/05/10/how-the-pentagon-started-taking-ufos-seriously.

O'Meara, Thomas F. *Vast Universe.* Liturgical Press, 2012.

Phenomenon, The. Directed by James Fox. Farah Films, 2020.

Rees, Martin and Donald Goldsmith. "The Webb Telescope Shows We Don't Need Astronauts to Explore the Cosmos." *The Wall Street Journal,* 21 July 2022, https://www.wsj.com/articles/the-webb-telescope-shows-we-dont-need-astronauts-to-explore-the-cosmos-11658419312.

Wilson, Eric G. *The Melancholy Android.* State University of New York Press, 2006.

7

STONE SECRETS OF THE GREAT LAKES

While searching for lost shipwrecks beneath the waves of Lake Michigan in 2007, an archeologist accidentally discovered a mysterious stone structure. On nearby Beaver Island, a cryptic stone circle was found in 1985. Obsidian rock unearthed from an ancient site at the bottom of Lake Huron in 2013 may be keys to prehistoric ways of life.

These are some of the tantalizing secrets held by the Great Lakes, and further exploration has unveiled some fascinating possibilities. The lakes, all connected in a continuous waterway, together form the largest collection of fresh water in the world. Thousands of wrecks lay scattered about the bottom of these inland seas, and tens of thousands have lost their lives in its deceitfully dangerous waters. In recent years, signs of early human activity have invited us to reexamine history, and have deepened the myths of our forebears. At the same time, the sheer natural beauty of the Great Lakes environment masks the unassuming mysteries that lie obscured.

The Grand Traverse Bay Stones

In the spring of 2007, professor of maritime archaeology Mark Holley led a team that used sonar technology to locate abandoned wreckage on the floor of Grand Traverse Bay, which is at the northeast end of Lake Michigan. He was successful in finding derelict boats and cars, but the most interesting discovery was a circular stone structure at about 35 feet below the surface. Upon further exploration, these stones seemed to have been positioned deliberately. Furthermore, the discovered structure was only a portion of a line of stones that extended for another mile (1.6 km).

One particular stone, about the size of a writing desk, is at the center of the prehistoric lore that pervades Lake Michigan. A petroglyph of what appears to be a mastodon graces its side, an exciting observation that some researchers believe helps to date the site. Since the mastodon became extinct about 10,000 years ago, the figure on the stone tells us that this structure is at least that old. That is, if the faded petroglyph is indeed that of a mastodon. Though archaeologists might debate this possibility, the stone shows how imagination at work in the present attempts to understand the past. Ancient stone formations such as these in some ways represent the continual struggle to find meaning in our place in the world. Through the Lake Michigan stones, we are afforded a fleeting glimpse of the people who walked the region thousands of years ago, humans who endured a world of glaciers as well as the birthing pangs of early organized society.

When word about the Grand Traverse Bay stone structure reached the popular media, it was mischaracterized as the "Lake

Michigan Stonehenge." Theories about the aquatic structure's esoteric purposes abounded in online articles and documentary shows. Although the lake stones may be visibly similar at a glance, England's Stonehenge is quite disparate. The structure beneath the waves is fascinating, without any extra magic associated with it. Its very existence speaks from a time before the land was literally inundated, prior to the recession northward of the great Laurentide ice sheet that covered much of North America. The best archeological conjecture is that the underwater stones acted as a hunting drive, where prehistoric hunters gathered to corner and attack caribou. These days, ships and sailboats pass over the surface of the lake, their passengers most likely unaware of the submerged revelations that lie below.

The Beaver Island Sun Circle

Only 38 miles north (61 km) of Grand Traverse Bay lies Beaver Island, recently described by one observer as an "idyllic summer getaway with a small population of 657." At the northern tip of Lake Michigan, the island's geographical location is directly in the midst of a historical gateway to the west. For hundreds of years, explorers crossed the waters of the Great Lakes on their way to the Mississippi River and beyond. Settlers have left written records and maps of the region, with early outposts dotting the shores of the lakes. Prior to that, indigenous peoples built communities here, from which artifacts continue to be excavated.

In 1985, retired teacher Terri Bussey was out on the western side of the island, engaging in a serious pastime. As she searched the area for Native American artifacts, she noticed among the stony terrain a particularly conspicuous boulder about the size of a kitchen table. On the top of the stone was an 8-inch indentation (20 cm), which was the first indication that the stone might be an unusual find. Examining some of the other stones in the immediate area, what appeared to be a petroglyph of feathers was found to adorn one of them. Not only that, but the stones seemed to have been arranged in a circular pattern, with a diameter of nearly 400 feet (121 meters). With 39 stones in all, the ring promptly spawned numerous theories as to their meaning. Bussey herself claims that the formation aligns with constellations, while other researchers believe it is a prehistoric calendar associated with the summer solstice.

Some geologists, however, insist that the sun circle is a product of natural forces. In this explanation, the stones are merely the lithic remnants of a prehistoric glacial lake's beach. Dating the stones has proven to be decidedly difficult, as various methods such as chemical analysis and archeological inspection have yielded no clues. Though there are anthropologists who suggest that Beaver Island was a kind of way station for early indigenous trade routes, possibly offering hints about the stones' history, the debate surrounding the structure persists. Local tribal elders conferring with Bussey believe that it may be a ceremonial site around 1,000 years old. Even if the position of the stones is a product of natural geological phenomena, they submit, it does not make the site any less sacred. Visitors are welcome to come and deliberate for themselves. Bussey says, "I hope it gives them a sense of wonder for the things that need to be looked at again and again."

The Lake Huron Enigma

According to archaeologist John O'Shea, what he found at the bottom of Lake Huron in 2013 challenges what we think we know about the human beings who lived there so long ago. At the time, his team of underwater researchers was excavating a discovery that in and of itself was already quite important. Along a submerged ridge that stretches across the lake, there lies evidence of an early campsite, complete with stone tools and campfire rings. Stone walls used as caribou hunting drives were also located. This ridge was last above water over 8,500 years ago, a time when monumental glaciers were still scouring the Great Lakes into their current forms. This means that the site, which is now 120 feet below the surface, must have once enjoyed lush flora and fauna out above the water.

The lakebed at the site is strewn with stone tools, wood, and bone. As one of the team members examined recovered samples, he noticed something strange. Shards of obsidian glass gleamed in the array, both shocking and puzzling the archeologists. They were proven to be cultural flakes, which indicates that they were shaped and utilized by humans. In the Great Lakes region, this was a thrilling rarity. How did these fragments of black volcanic rock end up in such an obscure spot? Further research determined that the obsidian originally came from a deposit in Oregon state, near the coast of the Pacific Ocean.

The stone hunting structures found in Lake Huron, coupled with the obsidian tools, provides a sharper picture of the deep past. Still, the enigma of how the Oregon rocks came to rest in the Great Lakes remained, until the pieces of this prehistoric puzzle were put together. O'Shea argues that the indigenous American peoples traversed the continent by far greater distances than previously thought. He believes that the unearthed obsidian made its way across the land in the hands of those who participated in vast and complex trade systems. These humans, then, interacted in sophisticated ways in their quest for survival in a harsh world.

The immense ice sheet that once covered the entire northern part of the continent, when pulled away by the eons, reveals a dimly occulted human past. These are the generations of men, women, and children who lived out their lives near the places we now call home. It captures the imagination to think back upon a time when the land was shaped differently than it is today. The water and stone hold their secrets tightly, and the deeper we go, the more we learn about ourselves. Though the ancient world might seem so long ago, it is important to remember that we are in fact not so far removed from our local ancestors. When thought of in terms of glacial time, it may as well have been yesterday.

Sources

"Archeologists believe a circle of boulders found on Beaver Island may have been a primitive calendar." *United Press International,* 19 June 1988.
https://www.upi.com/Archives/1988/06/19/Archaeologists-believe-a-circle-of-boulders-found-on-Beaver/1779582696000/.

C.,J. "Beaver Island 20CX65: The Other Lake Michigan Stonehenge." JaySea Archeology, 13 March, 2021.
https://jayseaarchaeology.wordpress.com/tag/beaver-island/.

C.,J. "The Enigma in the Lake: The Lake Michigan Stonehenge." JaySea Archeology, 24 Feb. 2021.

https://jayseaarchaeology.wordpress.com/2021/02/24/the-enigma-in-the-lake-lake-michigan-stonehenge/.

Martin, Aaron. "At the Bottom of Lake Huron, an Ancient Mystery Materializes." *Scientific American,* 1 June 2021. https://www.scientificamerican.com/video/at-the-bottom-of-lake-huron-an-ancient-mystery-materializes/.

"Mysteries of Lake Huron's Ancient Hunters Revealed." *Northern Michigan Conservation Network*, 29 April 2014. https://nmconservationnetwork.org/2014/04/29/mysteries-of-lake-hurons-ancient-hunters-revealed/.

O'Shea, John M. "Central Oregon obsidian from a submerged early Holocene archaeological site beneath Lake Huron." *PLOS One*, 19 May 2021. https://journals.plos.org/plosone/article?id=10.1371/journal.pone.0250840.

Randall, Brianna. "Archaeologists Have Found Prehistoric Rock Structures Under the Great Lakes. Here's What the Stones Can Tell Us." *Discover,* 23 March 2021. https://www.discovermagazine.com/planet-earth/archaeologists-have-found-prehistoric-rock-structures-under-the-great-lakes?fbclid=IwAR1kysMrgwTkZduUXXoFvRWcqZ0KMpcaX1XOw5nHm47fweJItSmqcENdhaU.

Soucek, Gayle. *The Lake Michigan Triangle.* Charleston: The History Press, 2022.

Sweitzer, Steve. "Lake Michigan Holds Ancient Secrets." *The Lasco Press,* 29 April 2019. https://www.thelascopress.com/2019/05/lake-michigan-holds-ancient-secrets/.

8

NO LONGER REMOTELY HUMAN

Throughout his renowned career in manga, Junji Ito has disturbed his readers with visceral tales of body horror and psychological dread. His characters often experience transformations, the product of inner demons that manifest themselves in physically monstrous qualities. Sometimes, however, social pressures work to compress characters' psyches to the point of collapse, whereupon mutation commences. Volume 7 of *The Horror World of Junji Ito* series, published in 1997, contains a story called "Slug Girl," a prime example of how this process occurs in Ito's storytelling. Soon after its publication, a story called "The Snail" appeared as a chapter in the work *Uzumaki,* a series which originally ran from 1998-1999. In that particular tale, an unusual young man is subject to peer aggressions that catalyze a disturbing metamorphosis. Each protagonist is a student set amidst the turmoil of adolescence, and each suffers a uniquely gastropodal horror.

From the very first panel of "Slug Girl," Yuuko's affliction is discredited before it even has a chance to show itself. As the titular girl, she is labeled "lazy,"[24] and by her supposed friend, no less, who is the story's narrator. Though it seems Yuuko has developed a speech impediment, this condition's association with laziness is tenuous. Her friend notes that Yuuko was once known for being talkative, but something has apparently changed. The narrator's unfair assumption is the first in a succession of subtle attacks on Yuuko's character, which quickly escalate throughout the early part of the tale. It is true that at first the narrator shows signs of concern for her friend, yet ultimately Yuuko's condition progresses beyond the point at which she can attend school in good health. Ito's haunting panel, showing her vacant desk, sets the tone for the emotional abandonment that is to come.

After some time, the narrating friend, whose name is revealed as Rie, pays a visit to Yuuko's home to check on her. Here is where the troubling gastropodal intimations begin. Yuuko's parents are in the back courtyard, violently fighting a slug infestation. Yuuko's father is seen stomping on the slugs, their gelatinous bodies flattened into two-dimensional outlines. Demonstratively destroying the creatures, his disgust will soon smoothly shift unto his daughter. Mother affectionately guides Rie to Yuuko's room, but once there, the pair is concerned to see Yuuko in bed with a facemask, Ito's trademark sweat beads excreting from her brow. Covering her face with her hands and unable to enunciate words, Rie offers what she might consider supportive solace. She says, "The doctor had only mentioned that your mental health is weak."[25]

---

[24] Ito, "Slug Girl."
[25] Ibid.

This statement is key, because it illuminates Yuuko's real problem: the prejudice and intolerance she has endured for being herself. Whether it be mental illness or a learning disability, the unfair qualifications of laziness and mental weakness directed toward Yuuko have erupted forth horror from within her. The changes in Yuuko would not be readily accepted by society, which values and encourages the "cheerful" and "chatty"[26] personality she heretofore exemplified. In a memory flashback, the reader learns that Yuuko was once, as a child, tormented with a slug by a classmate. She was essentially traumatized, for she subsequently never set foot in her family's slug-infested yard. Her terror never really left her-- not just that of the offending creature but of being the target of her peers.

In *The Body Keeps the Score*, psychiatrist Bessel Van Der Kolk outlines how trauma can manifest itself in various physiological ways, especially if not treated or if ignored by the individual. He explains that trauma can sap energy and motivation, as well as lead to "headaches, muscle aches, problems with your bowels or sexual functions," while including "irrational behaviors."[27] Alienation from peer groups, most especially during adolescence, is a trauma that Junji Ito explores with Yuuko (as well as with Katayama of "The Snail," but more on him later). The day after her initial visit, Rie is met with a revolting incomprehensibility: Yuuko's tongue has metamorphosed into a slimy, undulating slug.

How does best friend Rie react? By literally running away, never to return for another visit. Abandoned by her best friend and

---

[26] Ibid.
[27] Van Der Kolk, *The Body Keeps the Score*, 235.

met with revulsion instead of compassion by her own mother, Yuuko resorts to self-mutilation, a common coping mechanism of adolescent alienation and anxiety. However, slicing off the horrid appendage is to no avail, as it keeps growing back. Her father's take-charge attitude is coupled with hostility. He yells at his timid wife every chance he gets, clamoring for her to do this or do that in his blind focus to nullify the slug. This may at first seem like parental devotion and care. However, tellingly, the parents do not make an effort to actually understand what is happening with Yuuko. Rather, they endeavor to eliminate her affliction at all costs, even if that means possibly hurting their daughter in the process. After failed attempts to kill the buccal parasite, including a salt bath, the regenerating gastropod still lives. Yuuko's body has dissolved, save her head, which now acts as a protective shell, and she in essence becomes a snail. Tragically, social pressure to fit the mold has rendered her into a shell of her potential self. Yuuko's weary gaze in the last panel directly confronts readers, perhaps a challenge to consider someone like Yuuko in our own lives.

In "The Snail," an adolescent boy experiences cruel rejection by his peers, only to endure the emergence of his pain by way of physical transformation. Katayama, as he is called, develops these molluscan traits in response to his classmates' antagonism. As the story opens, students forlornly stare out the window during a torrential morning downpour. A student creaks open the door and reveals himself drenched not only rainwater, but in a viscous substance as well, as the careful detail in Ito's artwork suggests. Katayama only comes to school when it rains it seems, and straightaway his classmates start into their verbal assaults, targeting his slowness and apparent malaise. The teacher joins in the belligerence, admonishing Katayama for being late and also for not using an umbrella. According to an article in Comixology by Noah Berlatsky, Katayama's entrance scene is akin to a kind of birth, a "fertile source of horror" that emanates the "claustrophobic intimacy of a primal scene."[28]

Katayama's primary bully, Tsumura, uses the former's poor volleyball skills in gym class as the perfect opportunity to perform in front of his followers in malice. Katayama sees it coming, as an extreme closeup of his agitated face suggests. Tsumura, in a revealing moment, rebukes the antagonized boy for pleading with him in a familiar tone to stop the harassment, yelling, "Don't talk to me like we're friends!"[29] The insinuation of latent homoerotic anxieties continues as the bully cruelly strips Katayama naked and drags his body into the crowded hallway for all to see. Thus violated, his tormentor laughs, "Get a good look!"[30] The dehumanization of Katayama in this scene signals Ito's shift into body horror fiction, as a noticeable spiral appears on Katayama's exposed back.

The features of snail anatomy continue to develop as the rains subsist. As the spiral becomes a tumorous exterior growth, and Katayama's sliminess thickens, the classroom teacher only calls more attention to his deformity. Other characteristics forcibly emerge as Katayama becomes more socially isolated. He becomes not only marginalized but maligned into an outcast. In an essay

---

[28] Berlatsky, "Fecund Snails."
[29] Ito, *Uzumaki*, 240.
[30] Ibid., 241.

called "Creating the False Self," therapist Harville Hendrix concludes that traits not part of one's original nature "are forged out of pain and become part of an assumed identity" that "helps [one] maneuver in a complex and sometimes hostile world."[31] Katayama's full ostracization becomes finalized when he is confined to an outdoor pen, bulbous shell and tentacled eyes fully formed. He had escaped through the classroom window, vertically gliding on the side of the school building until violently knocked off with a broom. The group of students now a veritable mob, the organized expulsion of Katayama symbolizes their total and utter rejection.

Two girls somewhat sympathetic to Katayama, noticing that he has not emerged from his shell since the rain ended, splash water on his snail body. When his long eye appendages sprout forth, however, they run away screaming in revulsion. This is not unlike Rie's reaction in "Slug Girl." Soon thereafter, the bully Tsumura himself begins to transform. Once he is entirely transformed and also imprisoned in the pen, the two snails turn out to be attracted to each other. One of the girls comments, "Tsumura was such a bully. How ironic."[32] The class teacher reminds everyone that snails are hermaphrodites, as the two come together and apparently mate. Berlatsky writes, "There's a weird tenderness in the rapprochement between the two boy-snails, as they rest face to face with their phallic eyes intertwining."[33]

---

[31] Zweig and Abrams, *Meeting the Shadow*, 51.
[32] Ito, *Uzumaki*, 261.
[33] Berlatsky, "Fecund Snails."

Digging their way to escape, the two snails leave behind a slimy trail which is followed by the teacher and the two girls. Discovering a nest of eggs, the teacher remarks: "It's clear these two boys are no longer remotely human."[34] Certainly, each boy had subsumed within himself deep-rooted wounds that they managed in opposing ways. In Katayama's alienation and Tsumura's aggression, societal expectations are transgressed. The teacher violently stomps on the eggs and shrieks, "It's disgusting, it's unnatural!"[35] Recall that in "Slug Girl," Yuuko's father stomps on snails as his method of non-acceptance, a representative act of his inability to connect with his daughter and his refusal to acknowledge the changes in her life. In his article "Rejection and Betrayal," psychologist Robert M. Stein notes that when young people suffer these title experiences, "the more human personal relationship [will be] missing or inadequate"[36] in their lives. What is key is the concept that in the presence and aftermath of abuse, one's very humanity is compromised. With these stories, Ito demonstrates how the stripping away of his characters' capability to feel human yields to bodily corruption, an intensifying malignancy dense with suppressed shame.

One of the most troubling aspects of these stories is the parental rejection of Yuuko and Katayama. The reader is given a peek at the attitude of Yuuko's father when we first meet him in the yard, where he stomps away at the unwanted infiltrators. Exhausted by his violence, he commands his wife to bring him salt.

---

[34] Ito, *Uzumaki*, 264.
[35] Ibid., 265.
[36] Zweig and Abrams, *Meeting the Shadow*, 52.

Significantly, salt is also his suggested solution for curing Yuuko. Indeed, his approach is to fix his daughter, not heal her. He eventually eradicates her body in an outright rejection of undesirable characteristics, as it dissolves in a heavy salt bath while the head remains to serve as gastropod shell.

In Katayama's case, his parents call the school to inform his teachers that he has not come home for several days. This is understandable, apparently, for one teacher comments, "How could he go home looking like that?"[37] Ito's dark humor notwithstanding, the school asks Katayama's parents to come and collect him. However, once the father sees Katayama's new form, he exclaims, "That can't be our son!"[38] The horrified parents immediately go home in a quintessential example of parental refusal to acknowledge their child's identity. Now abandoned by his own mother and father, Katayama is a true pariah to all of society. While Yuuko is last seen pitifully gazing out atop a courtyard tree branch, Katayama and his new snail partner Tsumura are never seen again.

In 2020, Ito published a graphic adaptation of Osamu Dazai's 1948 novel *No Longer Human*, a work generally considered to be highly autobiographical. In Dazai's novel, the opening line to the protagonist's first-person narrative is, "Mine has been a life of much shame."[39] This statement, which Ito also uses as the beginning of his narrator's chronicle, serves as the nucleus of protagonist Oba Yozo's narrative. Ito's illustration of this quote is

---

[37] Ito, *Uzumaki*, 250.
[38] Ibid., 251.
[39] Dazai, *No Longer Human*, 21.

a panel of black ink, the text within a white egg-shaped figure, an indication that his shame is the point at which the rest of his life experience is birthed. In the first part of the novel, Yozo recounts the story of his early childhood, during which he suffers abuse and mistreatment at the hands of his classmates, his family, and their servants before learning to mask his dejection. The connection between Yozo's early life and the plights of the young characters in his manga work is not difficult to see.

Early in the novel, Yozo repeatedly but vaguely alludes to an unutterable "crime"[40] perpetrated against him by the servants, though the impression that he was sexually abused can be surmised. Ito, however, rather clearly represents these heinous acts in his adaptation. Yozo's confusion results in "painful wounds" that "unlike the scars from the lashing a man might give, cut inwards very deep, like an internal hemorrhage, bring intense discomfort."[41] While there is no real suggestion that his manga characters suffered similar sexual abuse, Ito's work is demonstrably concerned with the ways in which trauma can claim an individual's inner experience and transform it into something monstrous. In turn, their view of the outside world is paradoxically distorted through a lens of trauma while simultaneously opening a clear window into the horror of the cruelty of human beings. One such character in *No Longer Human* is the social outcast Takeichi, who, suffering from physical disability and possessing a uniquely cynical worldview, is "scorned by all."[42]

---

[40] Ibid., 38.

[41] Ibid., 48.

[42] Ito, *No Longer Human*, 43.

The main way Yozo manages his childhood distress it to become a "clown,"[43] whereby he outwardly pretends happiness and silliness in order to disguise his inner turmoil. He is able to skillfully fool all his friends and family, but Takeichi sees through him. Yozo, after making his schoolmates uproariously laugh at a tumble he takes in gym class, is confronted by Takeichi. He tells Yozo: "You did it on purpose."[44] This phrase haunts Yozo throughout the rest of the narrative, especially in the nightmarish and hallucinatory episodes of Ito's adaptation. The fact that an outsider is able to look so clearly into his psyche is an idea too much for Yozo to bear. His solution is to befriend Takeichi, who proves to have a visionary sense of reality's bleakness.

One day, Takeichi brings Yozo a self-portrait by Van Gogh, which he declares to be a picture of a "ghost."[45] Some artists, Yozo comes to realize, are the kinds of people "whose dread of human beings is so morbid that they reach a point where they yearn to see with their own eyes monsters of ever more horrible shapes."[46] Ito develops this theme throughout the adaptation, as Yozo becomes a visual artist whose chief goal is to represent the monstrousness of humanity. His influences are Van Gogh, Munch, Goya, and Modigliani, artists whose works often portray psychological pain. It can be easily imagined that Ito himself identifies with this vision.

---

[43] Ibid., 51.
[44] Ibid., 49.
[45] Ibid., 58.
[46] Ibid., 60.

In the novel, Yozo goes on to reflect that the great artists did not "hide their interest even in things which were nauseatingly ugly, but soaked themselves in the pleasure of depicting them."[47]

Eventually, Yozo's fear of intimacy grows as the two boys become closer, and because of this he perpetuates a cruelty unto Takeichi. In Ito's graphic version of the story, Yozo has an attractive cousin, and he makes Takeichi falsely believe that she admires him. When she shows her disgust toward Takeichi and vehemently rejects him, he kills himself. As an adult, Yozo himself attempts suicide by drowning with his lover, though he survives while she dies. On the morning of their suicidal act, Yozo reflects that his lover, like he, "seemed to be weary beyond endurance of the task of being a human being."[48] Some scholars have recognized Dazai's novel as a sort of literary suicide note, as the writer and his lover ended their own lives by drowning shortly after he finished the book.

An oft-cited influence of Junji Ito is writer Edogawa Rampo, whose collection *Japanese Tales of Mystery and Imagination* contains early stories of the grotesque and the perverse. The 1929 story "The Caterpillar" is one such example. The title itself is a precursor to the Ito manga titles discussed herein. The Rampo story revolves around a soldier who suffers terrible wounds in battle, resulting in amputation of all four limbs as well as an extremely disfigured face. Rampo writes, "In this monstrous face, however, there were still set two bright, round eyes like those of an innocent child."[49] In this

---

[47] Dazai, *No Longer Human*, 55.
[48] Ibid., 86.
[49] Rampo, *Japanese Tales*, 89.

way, the conflict between inner innocence and outer monstrosity is a thematic precursor to Ito as well. His wife is his caretaker, and although she seems to care for him at first, she gradually begins to torment him with little acts of teasing and then cruelty. The mutilated man ultimately escapes the house one night, gliding along on his belly before disappearing into a well in the ground.

Another notable tale that might be considered early body horror is that of Gregor Samsa. The famous opening line of Franz Kafka's novella *The Metamorphosis* sees the protagonist waking up transformed into a monstrous vermin, often imagined and depicted as a giant insect. Gregor's job as a salesman is strenuous, offering little respite from the tedious repetition of tiresome traveling. In other words, he is exhausted by the expectations of being an ordinary human in society. Intent on not leaving his bedroom in his insectoid form, Gregor's manager comes to the house to elicit him out. The manager says through the door: "I am dumbfounded, dumbfounded. I believed you to be a quiet, reasonable person, and now you suddenly seem intent on flaunting bizarre moods."[50] When Gregor is finally seen, his mother swoons and his father attempts to push him back into the bedroom. In a video analysis, one YouTube critic likens Yuuko of "Slug Girl" to Gregor Samsa, whose metamorphosis is a "desperate cry for help of someone who tries to express their struggles with depression and social anxiety in a time when mental illness literacy was practically non-existent."[51] This reading of the absurd tale complements the

---

[50] Kafka, *The Metamorphosis*, 128.
[51] YouTube, "Junji Ito's Slug Girl."

eventual abandonment of Gregor by his family. He dies alone, bereft of his humanity.

In an article titled "Black illumination," horror scholar Eugene Thacker writes that Junji Ito stories often take a "simple idea, which is then methodically inverted and perverted, until what results is a terrifying, mesmerizing, philosophical parable about the limits of being human."[52] The natural anxieties that plague the human being in the world, in Ito's stories, are exacerbated by the societal pressures around them. Osamu Dazai's protagonist asserts that society is nothing more than the collective struggles between individuals. As we see in Ito's work, these struggles can result in traumatic psychological distortion. Near the end of his graphic adaptation of *No Longer Human,* there is a metatextual twist when the author Dazai himself appears and meets his protagonist, Yozo. They seem to be virtually the same person, as Ito commingles perspective and dialogue. "For both of us," says Dazai to Yozo, "it's hard to keep acting out our comedy."[53]

Bibliography

Berlatsky, Noah. "Fecund Snails." Comixology. Rpt in. The Hooded Utilitarian. 31 Oct. 2011, https://www.hoodedutilitarian.com/2011/10/fecund-snails/.

Dazai, Osamu. *No Longer Human.* Translated by Donald Keene. New York: New Directions, 1958.

Ito, Junji. *No Longer Human.* San Francisco: Viz Media, 2017.

---

[52] Thacker, "Black Illumination."
[53] Ito, *No Longer Human,* 568.

Ito, Junji. "Slug Girl." https://imgur.com/gallery/HLC93ZP.

Ito, Junji. *Uzumaki*. San Francisco: Viz Media, 2010.

"Junji Ito's Slug Girl & the Horror of Being Different." *YouTube,* uploaded by RagnarRox, 15 March 2020, https://www.youtube.com/watch?v=d3iM8Xus8U.

Kafka, Franz. *The Metamorphosis, In the Penal Colony, and Other Stories.* Translated by Joachim Neugroschel. New York: Simon & Schuster, 1993.

Rampo, Edogawa. *Japanese Tales of Mystery and Imagination.* Translated by James B. Harris. Rutland: Tuttle, 2012.

Thacker, Eugene. "Black Illumination." *The Japan Times,* 30 Jan. 2016, https://www.japantimes.co.jp/culture/2016/01/30/books/black-illumination-unhuman-world-junji-ito/.

Van Der Kolk, Bessel. *The Body Keeps the Score: Brain, Mind, and Body in the Healing of Trauma.* New York: Penguin, 2014.

Zweig, Connie and Jeremiah Abrams, editors. *Meeting the Shadow: The Hidden Power of the Dark Side of Human Nature.* New York: Penguin, 1991.

9

We Dare You to Read!

The Censorship of EC Horror Comics

A decrepit wooden door slowly creaks open, revealing the interior of a dark vault. A yellow-eyed crone beckons you to enter with a bony finger. Behind her is a ghastly throng, watching and expectant. Hooded figures, horned humanoids, and hanging skeletons of the recently tortured surround a steaming cauldron. Skulls are strewn about, and a mangy rat scurries across the grimy floor. As a casket is pushed open by a grisly hand and bats thrash overhead, the Old Witch cracks a wry smile. A red signboard challenges you: "We dare you to read!"

This is the wonderfully macabre cover of the first issue of the EC Comics title *The Haunt of Fear,* and it brings me great joy. Published in 1950, Johnny Craig's cover art represents everything that EC horror comics stand for. It also reminds me of my teenage self, perusing the very small graphic novel section of my local library, and pulling off the shelf a hardcover copy of *Horror Comics of the 1950's.* It must have been the first time I laid eyes on the horror-happy hosts of EC. This compendium, collected a few decades after the heyday of EC horror, features a cover showing a man trapped in a mausoleum with a corpse. On the left side of the cover are the hideous visages of the three GouLunatics, from top to bottom: the Crypt-Keeper, the Old Witch, and the Vault-Keeper.

Though I had read a few horror novels at that young age, I was unprepared for the cornucopia of gleefully twisted stories and eye-popping images of EC horror. The book was filled with graveyards, animated corpses, and cackling madmen, which are some of the enduring EC themes and images. The more extreme fare, presented for the especially perverse among us, featured body mutilation, cannibalism, and gruesome death. Our three hosts laugh their way through it all, introducing the stories and providing narration. At the start of a tale called "The Thing from the Sea," the Crypt Keeper says, "Heh, heh. . . I see it's time for me to tell you another spine-tingling tale. . . one of my vast collection of chillers which I keep here in the crypt!"

Oh, to browse the Crypt-Keeper's library! That was my fantasy as a young fan of horror stories and weird tales. And there was no shortage of puns. The Old Witch, at the end of a story in which a man accidentally gets cremated alive, she says, "I'll try to have another heart-warmer next issue!" Readers of EC horror throughout the generations have felt a kinship with these three, and vice versa. The community of horror fanatics at the time (or Fan-Addicts), must have felt good to know that they were understood by the publishers of these comics, legends Bill Gaines and Al Feldstein. A case in point is a comment made in a letter printed in one particular Vault-Keeper's Corner, where the host tells a reader, "here you have what your diabolical little heart has longed for. . . fiendish fiction at its most macabre!"

Though the three hosts broke the fourth wall to welcome us to their story collections, the letters sections offered a chance for the hosts to speak directly to the reader outside the stories. In addition to the Vault-Keeper's Corner, we have the Crypt-Keeper's Corner and the Old Witch's Niche to entertain us with chronicles of their madcap rivalries. One could scarcely tell, however, which keeper could claim the Old Witch as his "ghoul-friend." In any case, it seemed she was successful in keeping the two at bay with her pointed insults and pun-filled jabs. Numerous letters from readers young and old were printed in these sections. Readers professed their love for the startling imagery and imaginative storytelling that were unique among comics at the time.

In the spirit of this feedback, the GhouLunatics were happy to provide book recommendations. The enthusiasm of the editors is strongly felt in their descriptions of what they call "fine mystery literature," adding that young readers' school or local librarians would surely assist them in acquiring these books. Some examples are Mary Shelley's *Frankenstein,* Robert Louis Stevenson's *Dr. Jekyll and Mr. Hyde,* and Bram Stoker's *Dracula.* The tales of Edgar Allan Poe are suggested more than once, which makes sense when realizing how noticeably EC horror comics were influenced by Poe.

Thus did the hosts provide a service by recommending texts that some saw as inappropriate for nice young ladies or young men in 1950s America. Certainly, there were school librarians and teachers who were allies in horror, but there were also parents and community leaders who believed these comics to be immoral. Although some of us can think back to at least one adult who understood our outlier interests, like-minded young people in the early 1950s did not have much support. In fact, they were vilified by a literal government investigation and grouped with criminals, all while their comic books were burned and the industry was virtually quashed.

The first issues of EC horror comics were published early in 1950, but despite their popularity and profitability, they were finished by the end of 1954. In the spring of that fatal year, psychiatrist Fredric Wertham published a book called *Seduction of the Innocent,* in which he argued that comic books contributed to juvenile delinquency. He reached this dubious conclusion after studying juvenile delinquents, some of whom apparently read comics.

Not only that, but he claimed that young readers of comics were being "seduced" by criminal behavior and suggestive sexuality, which could project mental disorders onto children. This type of ignorant and damaging rhetoric was quickly picked up by the media, which ran news articles praising the book, as well as new anti-comics ads. The horror and mystery comics published by EC were prime targets, with vitriolic editorials calling for their elimination. EC's "SuspenStories" titles such as *Crime* and *Shock,* the growing paranoia asserted, actually taught young readers how to be criminals. For example, an ad in the May 1954 issue of *Ladies Home Journal,* titled "What Parents don't know about Comic Books," reprinted a comics panel with the accompanying words:

"Every imaginable crime is described in detail. By teaching the technique, comic books also teach the content."

Parents across the nation were further whipped into a frenzy by a *Reader's Digest* feature called "Comic Books—Blueprints for Delinquency." Similarly, the *Hartford Courant* ran a campaign against comics titled "Depravity for Children—10¢ a copy!" The frontispiece pictured several EC titles, including *Tales from the Crypt, The Vault of Horror,* and *Mad.* The *Courant* had reached out to EC comics head editor Bill Gaines, seemingly offering him the chance to voice his defense. He was allegedly promised a balanced argument regarding comics. In the words of comics historian Grant Geissman, however, "no argument even remotely in support of comic books is to be found." The war on comics was swift, vicious, and entirely without merit. Besides the argument made by Wertham, there was no credible evidence that horror, mystery, and crime comics caused any detriment whatsoever to young readers.

Nevertheless, the anti-comics campaign caught the attention of U.S. Senator William A. Purtell of Connecticut. Comics were soon officially under investigation, with a special focus on the horror titles of EC. It is astounding to think that these books, which showcased classic monsters, strong storytelling, and groundbreaking artwork were viewed as a threat to the innocence of the nation. In April of 1954, hearings began for the Senate Subcommittee for "Juvenile Delinquency (Comic Books)." Rather than be accused of censorship of what they called a "filthy stream" of print, the purpose of the investigation was spun to "[awaken] parental responsibility and discipline." Bill Gaines appeared as a volunteer witness at the eventful two-day session, which took place on April 21ˢᵗ and 22ⁿᵈ. His mission was to defend horror comics.

Dr. Wertham, villain number one, was the first witness. His goal was clear, and that was to bring down the comics business. As long as the industry existed in "its present form," he stated, "there are no secure homes." The *Hartford Courant,* a leading paper in the anti-comics movement, erroneously and with fell purpose quoted him as saying, "as long as crime and horror comic books are published, no American home is safe." Significantly, the addition and emphasis of the word "American" struck a nerve with parents and citizens who were less than a decade removed from World War II. Their wartime trauma and fear were exploited by suggesting that these comics were somehow "anti-American."

When it was Bill Gaines' turn, he was aggressively questioned about an ad he printed on the inside front covers of his comics called "Are You a Red Dupe?" The ad shows a Soviet man printing a comic book when a government officer comes along to smash his printing machine, burn the comics, and summarily hang him from a rope. The caption beneath the 3-panel strip reads: "Here in America, we can still publish comic magazines, newspapers, slicks, books and the bible. . . we don't have to send them to a sensor first. Not *yet*." In this way, EC comics took a stand against what they viewed as pure fascism. In truth, there were a number of organized public comic book burnings that took place across the country in 1954.

Gaines' opening statement included a pointed dig at Wertham, saying "It would be just as difficult to explain the harmless thrill of a horror story to a Dr. Wertham as it would be to explain the sublimity of love to a frigid old maid." In order to make their case, the subcommittee brought forth several examples of comics art and storytelling, including the cover of *Crime*, which presents the head of a decapitated woman being held up by the hair. The man holding up the head is clutching a bloody axe in his other hand. Referring to this image, Senator Estes Kefauver asked Gaines: "Do you think that is in good taste?" To which Gaines replied, "Yes, sir, I do, for the cover of a horror comic."

Other spotlighted stories included ones in which characters suffered gruesome deaths, which the subcommittee deemed shocking and unnecessary. What they continually neglected to mention, however, is that these characters were often the malicious ones to begin with. The criminals, murderers, and greedy characters that populate EC comics commonly meet ironic and deadly twists of fate, emphasizing a karmic justice, or a kind of measure-for-measure morality. The little girl who shoots her father is the victim of terrible child abuse. The cheater who steals the family fortune loses it all. Killers often end up being killed themselves, usually in fitting ways, or haunted by their victims. Gaines did his best to fend off the onslaught during the hearings, but all of his words fell upon unsympathetic ears.

The New York Times ran an article about Gaines titled, "No Harm in Horror, Comics Issuer Says," causing further public damage. The veritable end of EC horror comics was nigh, as book distributors began returning issues in unopened bundles. After the hearings, Gaines continued his efforts to rescue his beloved industry, but the group of publishers he organized quickly realized that they either had to enter a long, unwinnable fight or acquiesce to some form of restriction. EC Comics stood to lose the most, however, since their bread and butter was horror. Bill Gaines, unwilling to compromise the work of his small but passionate team, quit the group that he had formed.

The group eventually went on to create The Comics Code, which was responsible for overseeing the suitability of comics publications for decades to come. Gaines called a press conference to announce the termination of his horror and crime line of comic books, and tore up a copy of *The Vault of Horror* to show how serious he was.

In the final issue of the *Haunt of Fear,* from December 1954, Gaines printed an "In Memoriam" page, detailing the finality of EC horror and crime but the inauguration of science fiction and adventure. His brief, sarcastic hope is worth the entire letter: "Naturally, with comic magazine censorship now a fact, we at E.C. look forward to an immeasurable drop in the crime and juvenile delinquency rate in the United States. We trust there will be fewer robberies, fewer murders, and fewer rapes!" In the final issue of *The Vault of Horror,* from January 1955, a weeping Old Witch declares her "Farewell."

In his introduction to the EC Archives series *Vault of Horror Volume 1,* author R.L. Stine discusses the magic of childhood discovery, when he first read a collection of EC comic books at his neighborhood barbershop. Stine describes the gist of these books: "at some point in every EC horror story, there is a scene so hideous, so ghastly, so bone-chillingly unthinkable that the protagonist must scream 'Good Lord!'"

The thrills and chills that these stories still elicit in modern readers is proven by the enduring popularity of well-produced new editions and formats, such as the archives series and the magnificent Taschen Books masterpiece *The History of EC Comics*.

The readers, writers, and publishers of horror owe remembrance to the EC generation of horror fandom and its allies. They fought for the right to tell a good ghastly tale. It is in this spirit that the current generation is now carrying forward a new golden age of horror. Horror literature reveals a dark, discrete side of human nature. It necessarily exposes the uncomfortable truths of the human condition alongside the era and settings that spawned them. All of us lovers of monster tales, slashers, body horror, weird lit, splatterpunk, bizarro fiction, and more, would willingly put up a fight to keep our stories— and some of us have done so. Like R.L. Stine noted, this fervor, once initiated, is forever a part of who we are. Long live the GouLunatics!

Sources

Chabon, Daniel, ed. *The Haunt of Fear Volume 1*. Dark Horse, 2021.

Chabon, Daniel, ed. *Tales From the Crypt Volume 1*. Dark Horse, 2021.

Chabon, Daniel, ed. *The Vault of Horror Volume 1*. Dark Horse, 2021.

Geissman, Grant. *Foul Play!*. Harper Design, 2005.

Geissman, Grant. *The History of EC Comics*. Taschen, 2020.

10

TO RAVISH & INTOXICATE

"You are the mighty ocean in the drop."

-Rumi

Preparation

In the transmission of thought, receptivity is paramount. With the creative act, the artist attempts to transcend conventional communication in order to express that which is otherwise conventionally inexpressible. Still, while one individual is moved by a work, another person is virtually unaffected. The former is receptive and sensitive to the transmission, while the latter is not conditioned to these qualities. The question of receptivity is applicable to the extreme live music performance. The more highly sensitive the listener, the higher the potential of direct consultation with the music. Furthermore, the more extreme the music, the more intense the rigor with which a listener must prepare.

Many traditions in mythology and religion, as well as theoretical physics, assert that in the very beginning of the universe there was silence accompanying darkness. Then there was the inaugural creative act-- whether conscious or not-- of introducing sound and light into the universe. The organism is in continual search for this reiteration: "Here darkness is not the absence of light (or of sound) but absorption into the outside."[54] It is this absorption into the outside that the listener of extreme music seeks to attain. In this way, the knowledge of the self is crystalized. With it often comes the height of ecstasy and the darkest of anguish, the entire spectrum of that which ought to be acknowledged and embraced by the devoted practitioner of the extreme.

The contrasting antitheses of silence and sound are fully realized in the live extreme music performance. The mind and body are receptive to thought when silenced in preparation for ritual. Extreme music is the object of awareness in this essay. Specifically, music of decimating and visceral sound. Music that induces terror and awe but ultimately resolves into a numinous state of being.

According to *Cult of Golgotha,* "All aspects of mundane life can be transformed into sacramental ritual acts."[55] The event of the live extreme music performance is a perfect candidate for prospective ritual, one that for the practitioner can lead to self-knowledge and a change of consciousness. The ritual process is an intentional outward display of inner thought and desire. Interestingly, the live show is a communal experience, adding to

---

[54] Georges Bataille, *Inner Experience,* p. 17
[55] Craig Williams, *Cult of Golgotha,* p. 119

the ceremonial nature of the event. However, it is contingent upon the individual to prepare their own receptivity. This preparation comes in the form of putting forth the time, effort, and work to increase lucidity and awareness of the object. These exercises in listening, previous to the live event, are the rigorous groundwork that eventually rewards a persevering devotee of the extreme. The ritual sequence serves as a tool for self-knowledge; it is a symbolic outward reaching for the scarcely attainable numinous state, and a means for the transformation of consciousness.

Lift the Veil

There is a moment at a live show in which the world of actuality can seem to fall away. In order to take part in the meaningful ritual experience, the audience member needs to create a mental environment that allows for this occurrence. At this point, this environment should have been formed by the aforesaid preparation. The preparation and readiness of the physical body to receive sound, wholly unimpeded by outside stimuli, is essential. The prepared sensitive mind can then be in a position to undergo a transformative experience, one that serves as a worthy contribution to the overall journey on a rigorous path to gnosis. The performance itself is merely one of the mediums through which negotiation of self-knowledge occurs. During the ritual process, the mundane environment will yield to high sensitivity. This sensitive state of mind catalyzes the reception of sound by mind and body.

Still, there is nothing supernatural here, as far as that term is traditionally employed. The ritual is always accompanied by awareness and acknowledgement. Musicians appear on stage, at once engaged in the role of presiders of ceremony. Entrance into the sanctuary of the performance space includes the gathering of gear, perhaps a word (perhaps not), and the onset of amplification hiss. Before the performance, the artist might present to the audience a moment of introspection. Acoustical elements of the space are registered by the perceptive listener. These elements coagulate into a pre-show dirge. This wordless monologue is emotive of the calm before the storm. We can remain in the current state because it is agreeable, although increasingly evocative of the obscurities from which much of extreme music originates. However, content stasis is not the intention of extreme music. These artists aim to push the live listener to a realm that would challenge sensitivity and transcend the here-and-now. During the dynamic transition from elemental particles of a performance to the storm of crushing chords and blast beats, the symbolic veil is lifted between mere perception and a deeper conscious awareness.

The moment the audience perceives the dirge give way to a mountain of sound is akin to the confrontation of one's miniscule place in the vast scale of physical space. This is the phenomenon of the sublime. The sublime is exemplified by the beauty and terror invoked by nature. The Romantic era artists sought to capture this feeling through their work. Poets, painters, and composers were all inspired by majestic mountains covered with rolling fog, vast forest chasms, and immense stormy skies. Extreme music, tonally and lyrically, is much concerned with exhibiting the quality of infinite expanse, and with the inspiration of awe. Amid the massive density of sound, the devoted listener confronts their own insignificance among the present immensity as well as the void's immeasurability. What follows is the "decapitation of the mind from the body and the relief from pain found beyond the veil."[56] The inside is absorbed into the outside, driving the mind far from the body and into the void. A fitting image is of the atom's rapid-expansion superimposition upon the galaxy.

Inside the Maelstrom

To reach this stage of experience is to have made a commitment. At this point, receptivity is high, and the rhythm of the show has been grounded. In extreme music, the challenge to the listener includes a plea for careful attention. The commitment of the listener is reciprocated by the artist, and herein lies the performer-audience bond that parallels the bond between priest and congregation, shaman and disciple, teacher and student, and countless other relationships of implied learning and trust. The extreme band skillfully uses the physical space of the performance to build on this connection, as in the use of the space to manipulate sound dynamics. The greatness of volume in extreme music contrasts with the negative intervals between this voluminous magnitude and the deep-rooted concept of primordial silence. Further developing this idea, the band responds to the conviction of an audience to add substance. This can range from the slowly building drone of instrumentation to the sudden violent eruption of full onslaught.

---

[56] David Peak, *The Spectacle of the Void*, p. 53

No matter the point on this spectrum of music presentation, the audience member is now wholly inside the maelstrom.

As a traveler might approach the outside rim of the forest, discover an opening, and enter within, the devoted listener prepares for the approach to the performance space, enters the sound in a symbolic lifting of the veil, and is fully embedded in the sonic sublimity. All sound is vibration, of course. Extreme music saturates the atmosphere with an intensity of vibration that is felt in bodily tissues. In this way, the audience member undergoes a submersion into sound that is both a mental and visceral involvement. The ancient Greek philosopher Longinus, in his treatise on the concept of the sublime, confers that the quintessential orator "seeks to ravish and intoxicate the audience" while on stage, "so that a grand conception may be instilled in the mind."[57] This motive is absolutely applicable to the extreme music artist and performer.

Another metaphor that represents this submersion into the intoxicating vibratory excess is a plunge into an ocean of sound. The surface is impinged, and the mind goes fully under water. How far one goes into the deeps is in some ways reliant on the push of the music's boundaries and the receptivity of the listener. It is then that the listener is confronted with the *tremenda majestas*. This is the raw feeling of majesty in the form of an absolute overpowering quality.

----

[57] Philip Shaw, *The Sublime*, p. 14

This feeling of being overpowered relates to the holy experience, opening up to "one's own submergence, of being but 'dust and ashes' and nothingness."[58]

Consciousness Obliterated

About two thirds of the way through a gong bath I attended, the sensation of levitation struck, one induced via the overload of soundwaves. In fact, the sound of the Tibetan gong arrested the attention completely, so much so that it rendered thought virtually incapacitated. The disintegration of stimuli was complete, and all that was left was the immersion of sound in all its power on the mind and body. It was as if the sheet of sound was a book, and the moment of sensory levitation a point of departure at which one could turn and pursue another world of knowledge. It was a metaphorical gateway that opened, similar to the veil being lifted between mundane awareness and an obscure consciousness-connectivity to deep time and the totality of the cosmos. It is this experience that the extreme music show can produce. Additionally, this moment brings to mind the idea that, in this state, "naked vision [is] seared by lucidity beyond its endurance."[59]

Endurance is an essential concept when approaching the ways to navigate the ritual of extreme music. The essence of the ritual here is communion. Rather than resist the intensity, volume, and heaviness of extreme music, one must open all reception input, in the same way that electricity flows into an amplifier.

---

[58] Rudolf Otto, *The Idea of the Holy*, p. 20
[59] Olaf Stapledon, *Star Maker*, p. 183

The impressionistic force of the sound will flood consciousness and impact the tissue of the body. Thusly, the question of endurance begins as an adversarial challenge but becomes an exercise in total communion with the energy of sound. Since the matter of the body is quite literally energy, the sharing of bodily intimacy with the sound produces an ecstatic effect. There exists a body of psychological knowledge of the effect of music on the brain and body. This includes its healing and restorative properties as well as its ability to trigger physiological reactions.

The overexposure to sound, such a common characteristic of the extreme live performance, results in a trance state for the receptive listener. The full weight of the act, in a category of music that is typically qualified as heavy, engenders a state of being not unlike religious ecstasy, or direct contact with the numinous. Another way to think about it is divine contemplation on a compressed scale. Accordingly, this event is like an act of purification through fire. What is left is the nucleus of the self, however ephemerally glimpsed: "Take courage now, and frail mortal though you are, try to understand yourself."[60] Significantly, this is an intentional directive, for control is the essence of ritual. In this way, the ritual of the extreme live show becomes sacramental. There is a clear change of consciousness that occurs, from material awareness to the nothingness quality of *tremenda majestas*. This temporary transformation, along with its permanent implications, is the experience toward which the devotee of the extreme aspires.

---

[60] *The Cloud of Unknowing*, p. 11

Therapeutic Brutality

There is an energy and drive in extreme music that is uncompromising. By this point in the ritual, the listener has been challenged to open the channel of input completely. Subsequently, a disintegration of mere perception takes place and a purity of awareness revealed. This disintegration is caused by the qualities of extreme music, including high volume and tempestuous instrumentation. Imagine the matter of the body broken down to the bits and particles that comprise it. In the spaces between lies the abyss of the organic form.[61] With this image, the energy and drive of the sound fully permeates the body. The extreme music artist projects the formal structures of sound that operate on the listener. In his book *Sacred Pain*, Ariel Glucklich discusses the notion that music creates patterns that correspond to the patterns of our mental and emotional inner lives. The intensity of the music is not unlike the apprehension of pain; the vigor with which the live extreme performer unleashes energy onto the listener finally leads to the contents of the world canceled out in the mind.[62]

In extreme music, formal patterns often push the listener to the limits of mind-body experience. For example, entire soundscapes are thrust into shuddering crescendos. Low frequencies produce reactions felt in the torso and the teeth. Vocals come from a dimension of animalism, wherein growls and screams tap the collective ecstasy and anguish of the human condition. Although this might seem like annihilation of the self, the author

---

[61] Thomas Ligotti, *Teatro Grottesco*, pp. 46-47
[62] Ariel Glucklich, *Sacred Pain*, p. 42

of *The Cloud of Unknowing* in fact qualifies this experience as self-awareness: there is an awareness of the self that brings joy and gratitude; there is an awareness of the self that brings agony and dread.

The uncompromising feature of the live extreme performance lies in its concentration. In the same way that compressed matter increases in density, the intensity of the sound feels like a massive wave. A high value is placed on the raw authenticity of the extreme artist, as the sound clenches itself into an agent of energy. It is an aural violence that is bereft of relief, and the ritual aspect here is a confirmation of one's place as a disciple of the extreme. Sound is a literal physical pressure wave whose presence can dominate consciousness. This idea is analogous to the extreme pain that dominates the attention field.[63] There is a therapeutic quality to the ritual engagement here, while the ferocity of sound surpasses the border between acknowledgement and transformation. Acknowledgement is of the mere perception of sound, and transformation the point at which consciousness changes. This change of consciousness is in many respects the very definition of sacrament. One result is a hypnotic effect. The relentless test of sonic endurance projected by the extreme musician often continues into a trance. In this way, the metaphorical fire of the extreme live performance has cleansed the listener of the mundane world's minutiae and has left only the nucleus of the self.

---

[63] Ibid.

Sacramental Paradox

In a psychological essay, Oliver Sacks describes how he personally connects to a moment in which, like a man in the midst of his own self-described madness, music suddenly and unexpectedly "pierced [his] heart like a dagger."[64] For Sacks, the music produces a stabbing pain that precipitates catharsis. One need not, however, suffer from the kind of grief Sacks was experiencing at the time to acquire the cathartic state. *The Cloud of Unknowing* author submits that the greatest suffering possible is to feel one's own existence. Whether or not the casual listener subscribes to this wisdom, the adept of the extreme is quite ceaselessly aware of this human condition. This awareness is juxtaposed with a conditioned sensitivity, one ripe for ritualization in the live extreme show. The dagger piercing the heart is an inherently violent image, but one that ignites a universal understanding.

Although it may seem paradoxical, the extreme sound which is analogous to pain releases the constant inner din accumulated in the ordinary world. It ultimately gives way to the numb nothingness of the sublime. An intellectual engagement ensues, one in which constricted thought is released (the unknowing) and the penumbra of gnosis glimpsed. Although some extreme aspects of the music can be a part of the presentation, it is crucial to keep in mind that these aspects do not necessarily derive from the lyrics, ideas, or imagery. Anyone can haphazardly proclaim these personal notions, but the artist formalizes and concentrates them into an

---

[64] Oliver Sacks, *Musicophilia: Tales of Music and the Brain*, p. 325

organized work. The extreme music artist, in this sense, uncompromisingly and deliberately destroys the limits of comfort and traditional acceptability. Too often, the uninitiated observer misrecognizes the nature of extreme music as unmitigated anger or aggression, depression or disorder. While of course these conditions might play a role, extreme music, as all artwork, can originate from any point of thought or feeling.

The extreme artist and dedicated listener are characterized by the willingness to respect the tradition, which is to push limits to the point of decimation-- and herein lies the ostensible paradox. The fierce thoughts and desires elicited by extreme music, and the subsequent transformation of consciousness, should be realized as a crucial goal of the ritual. Follow the current, and it will crystalize the simultaneous chaos and balance into revelation. One way to deepen and widen consciousness, according to Carl Jung, was to concurrently hold the extremes of light and dark in our own hearts.[65]

The ritual of the extreme live music performance, then, constitutes what Zweig and Abrams call shadow-work. This includes "peering into the dark corners of our minds." Jung continues by declaring that "long and difficult negotiations will be unavoidable."[66] In this sense, the ritual serves as a difficult negotiation, and resolves in a canceling out of the mind, leaving the naked inner self. Here the initiate accepts the apparent heresy which is the truth taken to the extreme.[67] Within the ritual, the

---

[65] Zweig and Abrams, *Meeting the Shadow,* p. 271
[66] Ibid.
[67] Michael Casey, *Sacred Reading,* p. 105

role one plays is a symbolic demonstration of the desire for knowledge. The adept conducts itself toward the extreme with this idea in mind. Another ritualistic feature is that both performer and listener employ metaphorical temporary masks in order to become concentrated forms of themselves. Imagine the mask as a way to present the true self. Although the mask obscures the outward appearance of the individual, it simultaneously allows the individual to act according to its true nature. Richard Gavin affirms that "as paradox-process, the ritual employment of masks is a superlative conduit toward the soul's unfathomable reaches."[68]

Reverberation

The ritual of live extreme music will deeply penetrate the sensitive and prepared listener, for "the true abyss has turned out to be human beings."[69] A dive into those depths is the responsibility of all devotees of the extreme, as well as all students of the esoteric. For artist and listener, notes A.J. Dunning, extremes speak of aspirations that transcend the personal and challenge the sanity of standard human behavior.[70] Truly, 'standard' should never define the world of the authentic extreme artist. In music, this is the live artist that relentlessly challenges the listener to the point of a change in consciousness, and in special moments will deliver it to transcendence. Although this article is concerned with live music, the same goes for all forms of art and text.

---

[68] Richard Gavin, *The Benighted Path*, p. 101
[69] A.J. Dunning, *Extremes*, p. 3
[70] Ibid.

Often, it is the mental endurance and visceral stamina that qualify the extreme live show that reverberates in one's consciousness for days afterward. Ephemeral though the numinous state may be, its echoes comprise the currents that outwardly emanate from the enhanced listener. Permanence takes the form of learned self-knowledge, whatever shape that assumes for the individual. To borrow from the horror of philosophy, the ritual of extreme live music "also manages to be mystical at the same time that the individual performer is dissolved into a meshwork of tones- voice, space, and instrument variously existing in consonance and dissonance with each other."[71] This description is apt. The listener within the venue space for the duration of the show departs altered.

Imagine the leaves of black tea steeped in hot water. As the clarity of the water becomes endarkened, so the flavor and strength of the tea is augmented. Exiting the space of the live venue should result in a similar transformation. The event will have served as an essential contribution to permanent knowledge. In this sense, once ritualized, the show will have marked a notch on the path of the individual, one as recognizable as any learned text might add, and as deep as a sacramental act.

Bibliography

Bataille, Georges. *Inner Experience.* Trans. Leslie Anne Boldt. Albany: State University of New York, 1988.

---

[71] Eugene Thacker, *In the Dust of This Planet,* p. 21

Casey, Michael. *Sacred Reading: The Ancient Art of Lectio Divina.* Liguori: Harper Collins, 1995.

Dunning, A.J. *Extremes: Reflections on Human Behavior.* Trans. Johan Theron. New York: Harcourt Brace Jovanovich, 1992.

Gavin, Richard. *The Benighted Path.* Munich: Theion, 2015.

Glucklich, Ariel. *Sacred Pain: Hurting the Body for the Sake of the Soul.* New York: Oxford University Press, 2001.

Ligotti, Thomas. *Teatro Grottesco.* London: Virgin, 2008.

Peak, David. *The Spectacle of the Void.* USA: Schism, 2014.

Sacks, Oliver. *Musicophilia: Tales of Music and the Brain.* New York: Vintage, 2008.

Shaw, Philip. *The Sublime.* New York: Routledge, 2006.

Stapledon, Olaf. *Star Maker.* Mineola: Dover, 2015.

The Cloud of Unknowing. Ed. William Johnston. Garden City: Image, 1973.

Otto, Rudolf. *The Idea of the Holy.* Trans. John W. Harvey. London: Oxford, 1958.

Thacker, Eugene. *In the Dust of This Planet.* Alresford: Zero, 2011.

Williams, Craig. *Cult of Golgotha.* Montreal: Anathema, 2018.

Zweig, Connie and Jeremiah Abrams, Eds. *Meeting the Shadow: The Hidden Power of the Dark Side of Human Nature.* New York: Penguin, 1991.

11

PHANTOM LANDS

In his 1923 book *New Lands,* Charles Fort, the occult researcher and chronicler of bizarre phenomena, wrote of eerie visions. These mystifying appearances include mirages of unknown landscapes, cities floating in the sky, and ghost armies marching in the vague distance. The majority of reports in *New Lands* transpired throughout the 19th century and into the early 20th century. This era saw the rapid development of telescopes and astronomy, which inevitably led to delusional events such as the Great Moon Hoax of 1835 and the Martian canals debate later in the century.

The discovery of geological time and the advent of particle physics further contributed to the idea that there were mysteries beyond the ken of civilization. Contrary to tradition, the nature of reality was actually not as it seemed, a concept simultaneously exhilarating and terrifying. These blossoming impressions manifested themselves in early science fiction literature and weird fiction, genres that show us worlds beyond the veil of our mundane reality.

Three exemplary stories published in the decades leading up to the Fortean period exhibit enigmatic locales. In each of these stories, characters enter into otherworldly realms, phantom lands whose ethereal beauty is dreamlike and intoxicating. Robert W. Chambers' 1895 story "The Demoiselle d'Ys" features a lost hunter unexpectedly transported to past times of falconry and medieval courtly love. In H.G. Wells' 1906 story "The Door in the Wall," a man is haunted by a strange childhood visit to gardens of harmony and delight. Lastly, Lord Dunsany's 1916 story "The City on Mallington Moor" tells the story of a rumored, fantastic metropolis that is said to emerge from the secluded mists.

Philip, the hapless narrator of "The Demoiselle d'Ys," finds himself lost among what he calls "somber moors" at the start of his story. He realizes that his strange surroundings preclude his finding the way back home before nightfall. Something in the air tells him he is in "a bad place for a stranger." The concept of a strange sort of intuition permeates each of these three stories; something is not quite right, and it is something more indirectly perceived than directly felt. The feeling is an ambiguous cognitive alert that something in the fabric of reality has shifted. In his book *The Super Natural,* Whitley Strieber affirms his belief that "our material culture explain[s] away phenomena that are in some way real, but which have so far eluded understanding."

Chambers' collection *The King in Yellow,* in which this story first appeared in 1895, is a paramount example of early supernatural fiction. Important to note is that the ever-growing industrial materiality of the late 19th century can be seen as a fundamental influence on weird literature's beginnings, including these stories. As Philip accepts the fact that he will need to camp in the wilderness for the evening, he is confronted with the sight of a magnificent falcon capturing a hare. This astonishing vision is accompanied by a young woman, the demoiselle Jean d'Ys, who leads him into the woods before the two fall in love. As such, Philip cannot bring himself to leave the woman's mysterious castle in the woods, and before long he feels comfortable with riding and falconry, often out under the moorlands' "ghostly sheet of mist."

Still, Philip continues to sense an "undefinable" element to it all. In the end, he is bitten on the ankle by a poisonous snake, and he swoons. Upon waking, the ethereal world is gone and his normally-perceived reality is back. A dead snake is in the grass, and nearby is a forlorn gravestone proclaiming the 16th-century demise of Jeanne d'Ys, who died of a broken heart for her lost stranger, Philip. The young woman's warm and fragrant glove is found upon the stone, suggesting that the liminal space between dimensions is quite fragile.

William Faulkner once wrote, "The past is never dead. It is not even past." In this way, the fluidity of time in these stories adds to their dreamlike quality. It is also a reminder to readers that we have all experienced the nebulous quality of time at some point in our lives. Lionel Wallace, the experiencer in Wells' "The Door in the Wall," exclaims to his confidante that he feels "haunted." As he narrates his story, we learn that he is not haunted by a ghost, exactly, but by a memory of bliss. As a child, a mysterious green door would appear to him, one that he could see but that no one else seemingly could.

He felt powerfully attracted to it, yet repelled at the same time, as if something beautiful yet dangerous lay beyond that door. When he finally plucked up the courage to open it, the paradise beyond the wall was staggering.

Compared to the harshness of the regular world, the peace and tranquility of the garden utopia beyond the door is almost too great to bear. This sentiment would have no doubt resonated with readers of the time, as it still does today. Placed within Lionel's strict childhood and workaday adulthood, the enchanted garden serves as an escape from the din of industrial civilization. In his book *Hauntings,* psychologist James Hollis writes about how we have all desired to escape the "steady drumbeat and reiterative abuses of daily life."

Wells presents readers with the prospective question: what if we could merely open a door and leave all our stress and responsibility behind? Though the temptation to stay in that ethereal garden world was immense, Lionel was able to get back out, unable to fathom leaving his young life behind. The door continued to present itself to him throughout his life, however, and he somehow knew that the next time he entered he would never leave, for he had been haunted by "unforgettable and unattainable things." The story ends with the vanishing of Lionel Wallace. Had there ever been an actual door, muses the narrator? Or, did he seek the security of death's darkness as an ultimate relief from the relentless modern world?

In *The Moribund Portal,* Richard Gavin writes that "ghostly infusions of the land billow between worlds, that of the grosser material plane and that of immaterial numen which infuses material forms." Lord Dunsany's "The City on Mallington Moor" certainly evinces this idea, through a numinous encounter out in the British countryside. The narrator of the story begins his journey by tracking down an old shepherd who is said to have glimpsed a fantastical city on the moor. Notably, the narrator initially goes out to the country as a respite from the crushing weight of urban society, a common thread in these stories.

In effect, this is a story of psychogeography, where the environment shapes the narrator's wandering, which eventually leads him serendipitously to a "queer old inn." The locals there had been dismissive of the old shepherd, and were somewhat amused rather than intrigued by his alleged visions. At length the narrator finds the lonesome shepherd out on the moors, and shares his whiskey with him as a token of good faith. While the shepherd is at first reticent about sharing his visions with a stranger, he concedes when the narrator seems genuine in his interest. The old shepherd later points the way to the mysterious city, down a faint track in the ground, which itself is "no more than the track of a hare—an elf-path the old man called it, Heaven knows what he meant." Once beyond the horizon, the narrator gives up hope of finding the city and lies down to rest. He immediately is met by a thick cloud of mist, described as a "long high wall of whiteness with pinnacles here and there thrown up above it, floating towards me silent and grim as a secret."

Enveloped in the abrupt mist, the "different rules of nature" prevail, in the words of Whitley Strieber. The narrator then falls asleep after emptying a flask that the shepherd gave him, one with "strange strong rum, or whatever it was." Upon waking, he follows the twisting track to a wide depression in the land, where the "mist flapped away like a curtain," revealing the majestic city on Mallington Moor. The narrator is stunned by its edifices of "pure white covered with carving," marble terraces, and towers topped with gold. Kindly people tell each other stories and play gentle music on balconies in this wonderful place where "there was none of that hurry of which foolish cities boast." The narrator is intoxicated by the music and falls asleep near a sign reading "Here strangers rest." When he awakes the city is gone.

James Hollis writes that "our predecessors considered the contiguous boundaries between visible and invisible worlds highly fluid, highly permeable." This concept has returned to our own world through a recent legion of imaginative writing and art. It was disillusionment with modernity that ignited the writing of the stories in this article, much in the same way that our present state of societal turmoil has given rise to new and diverse modes of artistic form and expression. We continue to adapt to novel methods of communication and media, which impact our collective consciousness in unexpected and unpredictable ways. As the weight of our own postmodern civilization grows heavy with crises, we adjust. As current discord and intolerance spreads, we do what we can to contain the fire. At the same time, we create new stories. We seek and find respite in our books and art, in our zines. In our own phantom lands.

Bibliography

Chambers, Robert W. *The King in Yellow*. Dover, 1970.

Dunsany, Lord. *Wonder Tales*. Dover, 2003.

Fort, Charles. *New Lands.* Ace, 1973.

Gavin, Richard. *The Moribund Portal.* Three Hands Press, 2018.

Hollis, James. *Hauntings.* Chiron, 2013.

Strieber, Whitley and Jeffrey Kripal. *The Super Natural.* Penguin, 2016.

Wells, H.G. *Selected Stories of H.G. Wells.* The Modern Library, 2004.

12

Life's But a Poor Player

Character

Lady Macbeth has just been found dead, evidently by suicide. Macbeth is told about his wife's death at a time of turmoil, as Macduff's army is approaching Inverness, Macbeth's castle. Overall, things are not exactly turning out the way he planned.

Although he had wavered in his own thinking about taking the crown from King Duncan, his wife had, with her strong sense of purpose, convinced Macbeth to murder the king. Thereafter, he had his good friend Banquo killed out of selfishness, and has been suffering the guilt and madness that came along with this despicable act. To complicate things, the obscure prophesies of the witches are always in the back of his mind. It is at this moment when Macbeth delivers a speech that reflects his despair at his own discovery of life's fragility and meaninglessness: "Life's but a walking shadow, a poor player/ That struts and frets his hour upon the stage/ And then is heard no more." [2]

In his declaration that "life's a poor player," he suggests two notions. One is that life is a player, and a poor one at that. In other words, our lives consist of merely acting a certain part, whether it is conditioned in us, or a conscious type of acting that is informed by the social or cultural values around us. However, it is "poor" because, in the vast scheme of the entire world, the acting of a single player cannot have any meaningful or far-reaching significance.

Secondly, among the possible identities it can claim, life is only a poor player. This is to say, it is not a king, queen, dignitary, and certainly not a god. Life is not particularly special, for a poor player is not very high up on the social ladder. In fact, the life of a player is made up of *pretending* to be other people. The player is not the real thing itself, but only a "walking shadow" of the real thing. In Macbeth's own mind, it is difficult for life to compete with the everlasting phenomena of time and death. He says, "all our yesterdays have lighted fools/ The way to dusty death." [3] The purpose of his actions is now called into question.

Of course, he had been inwardly conflicted about his own ambition, but the finality of Lady Macbeth's death has struck the chord of guilt and regret. In the face of the recognition of the insignificance of life and its events and actions, Macbeth plays the part of introspective philosopher- as to what degree of sincerity he may have achieved; it is up to the reader to decide. Therefore, he himself has become a player, an idea intensified even more with the immediately ensuing part he takes on, that of a raging bully who threatens a messenger that comes in with the inconceivable news that Birnam Wood is itself physically approaching the castle.

To complicate things, however, it is quite possible that Macbeth presents himself to *his own self* in uttering these words. For example, if Macbeth can convince himself of his own metaphor (that life is indeed a poor player), and that the events and actions therein are lacking in meaning and substance, then his own actions are much more palatable. He can then imagine that in the broad scheme of things he is not required to justify his now seemingly inconsequential actions. Time and the world will go on, in other words, despite the results of his own diminutive circle of life. The guilt he may feel for the deaths of Duncan, Banquo, Macduff's family, and now Lady Macbeth, is pointless. So, in verbalizing his awareness that life is a "brief candle" that "signif[ies] nothing,"[4] he can extricate himself from the burden of responsibility.

Harold Bloom presents yet another element to this idea of Macbeth's performance to himself. He notes the connection between the "shadow" of his speech and his later statement: "I'gin to be aweary of the sun,/ And wish th'estate o' th' world were now undone." [5] He explains that just as the shadow cannot survive the disappearance of the sun, the player on the stage cannot survive the disappearance of the audience member. This concept provides an excellent opportunity for students to further explore the relationship between performers and audience members as it applies to the 'player' aspect of the performance triangle. First of all, one can not exist without the other. Performer and audience member are mutually dependent on one another.

An inevitable question is, "what is it about a performance that draws an audience member emotionally into a play?" In reality, audience members know that the characters on stage are not 'real' people, and the art director, no matter how skilled, cannot duplicate the setting the way, say, a film can. Still, a good performance can have an effect on a willing audience member; and therein lies the key. An audience member is willing to accept all that is present to him or her, and suspension of disbelief goes a long way in the hands of skilled actors. Therefore, in their staged reading activities in this unit, students should be mindful of this performer-audience member relationship.

In this Scottish play, there are persistently layers of meaning embedded in the language that a character speaks. Earlier in the play, Macbeth and Lady Macbeth argue about the prospect of murdering Duncan. The dialogue in this entire scene is another example of the central concept this curriculum unit will focus on; that Shakespeare's characters, like us, tend to play a part, presenting themselves in a role in order to convince others of the sincerity of that role. In this scene (Act I, scene 7), the turmoil within Macbeth's mind is apparent. As the scene opens, Macbeth delivers a soliloquy in which he debates whether to murder Duncan. After examining the risk, coupled with the fact that Duncan, who is a guest in his home, is a virtuous king, he seems to have decided not to let his ambition drive him to disreputable deeds. He begins, "If it were done when 'tis done, then 'twere well/ It were done quickly." The possibility of the murder is still present in his mind at this point, but he counters himself during his interior deliberation a few lines later: "as his host,/ [I] should against his murderer shut the door,/ Not bear the knife myself." [6]

Before he completes his soliloquy- for Shakespeare makes this clear with a dash to end the speech- Lady Macbeth interrupts.

There is a notable shift in tone from his soliloquy to his instant declaration to his wife that they "will proceed no further in this business." This shift and then the maintaining of this tone is violently broken in on by Lady Macbeth and the gruesome imagery she uses to persuade her husband that their original plan to depose the king should be followed through. She also insults him and calls his manhood into question: "When you durst do it, then you were a man;/ And to be more than what you were, you would/ Be so much more the man." Here, Lady Macbeth delivers a remarkable performance herself. She presents herself as a forceful, uncompromising individual rooted in determination. She chooses not to show her own inward thoughts of frailty as a woman. Yet, she does outwardly expresses these thoughts to the audience in her speech: "Come, you spirits [. . .] unsex me here,/ And fill me, from the crown to the toe, top-full/ Of direst cruelty." [7] She implores the spirits to change the fundamental femininity about her; she desires to become something else. In essence, she desires to assume a different role with the intention of presenting that *self* to the outside world, just as an actor will call on the muse to help better create a character upon the stage.

Self

Most of Shakespeare's characters are reflections of, and reflective of, people we know in our real lives. They also remind us of ourselves- for who has not, as Macbeth does, carried on an internal debate when a tough decision lies before us? Who has not presented themselves, as Lady Macbeth does, as more confident, and less vulnerable, than they really were at the time?

As we live our daily lives, we tend to play multiple roles, whether consciously or not. The fact that people present themselves as they want others to perceive them is a common element of human behavior. Individuals perform, so to speak, to the outside world in a sometimes very calculating way.

This concept is the main argument of Irving Goffman in his sociological work *The Presentation of Self in Everyday Life.* He argues that individuals have an internalized sense of whom or what they are, and how they must represent this sense to outside observers. However, this internalized sense of self is continuously shifting, so that the presentation of the self may be drastically different in separate circumstances. The part that individuals play for others is much like an actor what an actor does in taking on a role for an audience. Just as the actor's challenge is to convince the audience to take him seriously as the character he is portraying, individuals endeavor to convince their observers of a particular persona. In doing so, people must attempt to maintain that persona- which itself is a performance. Goffman sums up this idea by saying that individuals, whilst performing, hope that outside observers "believe that the character they see actually possesses the attributes he appears to possess, that the task he performs will have the consequences that are implicitly claimed for it, and that, in general, matters are what they appear to be." [8]

Goffman goes on to argue that not only do individuals perform for others, they perform for themselves. He discusses two key extremes that the individual may experience. On one hand, a performer can be completely convinced by his own performance.

This scenario is not unlike the circumstances in which Macbeth finds himself in as he internally debates whether to let his ambition dictate murderous action. If the performance is successful in persuading the individual of this selfhood, then it may be possible to justify any action or behavior.

On the other hand, Goffman continues, the individual, in performing for himself, may not be convinced at all. He notes that this is "understandable, since no one is in quite as good an observational position to see through the act as the person who puts it on." [9] This may seem obvious, but it truly is an extraordinary insight. Through the character of Macbeth, Shakespeare heightens our awareness of the relationship between outward and inward performance. Lady Macbeth herself offers us distinct voices, and, consequently, distinct performances. It is this relationship between the self and the ways in which we distinguish outward and inward presentations that focuses the reading of Macbeth in this unit. Students will begin by examining their own *selves*, and questioning preconceived notions of what makes up their own selves in relation to how they perform in their everyday lives.

Player

Between the concepts of Macbeth's performances within his play and the self-performances of individuals in the real world, lies another paradigm of performance; that of the player, or actor. In this unit, students will come to a deep understanding of the overarching phenomenon of performance by studying the ways in which actors play parts in Shakespeare. In high school classrooms, much effort is directed toward supporting students with visuals such as video clips or illustrations. Audio clips of plays also give students an insight into ways in which actors and directors interpret the text.

Actors have been performing Shakespeare for hundreds of years now, and the countless approaches to Shakespeare's characters have been chronicled. In the case of the characters in *Macbeth, a* great opportunity arises in which to interpret a character with multifarious voices and presentations of self. In his book *The Player's Passion,* Joseph R. Roach recounts the ways in which actors throughout history have attempted to embody the psychology of their characters. As the field of modern psychology developed in the late nineteenth century, it gave actors more fuel for their approaches to acting. [10] In light of this, *Macbeth* lends itself exceptionally well to the study of performing character. Shakespeare affords us plenty of opportunity to interpret the characters' words and behavior in order to come to understandings about these characters' psyches.

In discussing *Macbeth,* Marjorie Garber insists that "interpretation and its risks and dangers are at the heart of the play [. . .] equivocation in Shakespeare's time was associated with the Jesuit practice of 'mental reservation'- saying one thing while holding in reserve another, more private thought or belief." [11] This idea of mental reservation is epitomized by Lady Macbeth's plea to her husband that he 'look like the innocent flower, but be the serpent under't."

Things are made all the more interesting considering the fascinating history of the productions of *Macbeth.* Garber explains the disaster-prone and volatile history of the play's productions, leading many actors and directors to deem it cursed, even to this day. The connection between text and stage is bridged by the actor, and students will discover this in exercising staged readings. Still, the interpretation and analysis of *Macbeth* need not be staged for an audience. Silent readers may also 'hear' the inflection, tone, and delivery of the characters in their own minds. It is the challenge of the actor to transmit this performance from the mental to the physical, making it manifest for audiences along with the communication of body language. All in all, the character-self-player paradigm pervades this most dark and turbulent of works.

Sources and Further Reading

Bloom, Harold. *Shakespeare: The Invention of the Human.* Penguin, 1998.

Garber, Marjorie. *Shakespeare and Modern Culture.* New York: Pantheon, 2008.

Gibson, Rex and Janet Field-Pickering. *Discovering Shakespeare's Language.* Cambridge: Cambridge, 1998.

Goffman, Irving. *The Presentation of Self in Everyday Life.* New York: Doubleday, 1959.

Roach, Joseph R. *The Player's Passion: Studies in the Science of Acting.* Ann Arbor: University of Michigan, 1993.

Rosenberg, Marvin. *The Masks of Macbeth.* Berkeley: University of California, 1978.

Shakespeare, William, and Sylvan Barnet. *Macbeth.* New York: Signet Classics, 1998.

Wilders, John, ed. *Shakespeare in Production: Macbeth.* Cambridge: Cambridge, 2004.

13

THE MUCK-ENCRUSTED MOCKERY OF A MAN

Part I

All of Infinity Within One Gigantic Instant

Encountering the climax of *Swamp Thing* #62 is a mind-expanding exercise. Our narrator, Metron, recounts how he and the Man of Muck encounter an aleph. Throughout the story, Metron is on a mission to attain The Source, which seemingly promises the meaning of all existence. He instead unintentionally confronts an aleph.

Through this aleph, he sees the totality of all action and information in existence. Information and meaning are not the same thing, however. This is something that Darkseid would agree with, for he mocks Metron for believing he had actually consulted with The Source. Indeed, we discover from Darkseid himself that what Metron and Swamp Thing negotiate while traversing the cosmic expanse is actually an aleph, which he defines as a point "from which one can observe all other points in time and space." This challenging concept stretches the imagination. Attempting to describe the aleph experience, Metron pauses the drive of his narration to offer this rhetorical question: "How does one convey the act of seeing all of infinity within one gigantic instant?"

It is interesting that while Metron seeks the meaning of all life and existence, he instead discovers only information and actions. It seems that even with the god-like power to know everything that happens, meaning itself is still elusive. The artistic layout for the climactic scene parallels the nature of the overwhelming encounter with the aleph. As Metron and Swamp Thing are confronted by the immensity of all things, the reader encounters a nine-panel framework, which then opens into a staggering two-page spread of thirty-two panels. Each panel represents a glimpse of some part of the universe. Some are profound, like the majestic galaxies; some are quotidian, like an open country road sometime in the remote past. Still, each panel is given equal weight and size. It is as if each action in the universe, regardless of time, has its place in the workings of the cosmos.

One panel is particularly curious. It is a closeup of a man's face. He has whitewashed eyes and a cigarette hanging from his mouth. In the foreground is the top portion of a typewriter, while the open shutters behind the man open onto a view of tall city buildings. The caption, quoted straight from the mouth of Metron, reads: "In a garret in Buenos Aires, I sat typing with a genius, blind twenty years." This man, of course, is the writer Jorge Luis Borges. We can only presume that he may be in the act of composing one of his most beguiling short stories: "The Aleph."

The narrator of this Borges story recounts how he comes to associate with a man named Carlos Argentino Daneri, a self-described epic poet. He is currently in the process of writing a long poem called "The Earth," which is about the world and everything in it. The narrator, however, considers his poetry to be drivel. Later in the story, the poet confesses as to how he actually gets his grand ideas about life and the world. In his cellar, so he claims, is a hidden point of light that manifests itself from out of nothingness. When gazed upon, says the poet, "without admixture or confusion, all places of the world, seen from every angle, coexist." Darkseid himself couldn't have described it better. Our disbelieving narrator, out of curiosity, agrees to see the aleph for himself. And yes, to his confoundment, it's real. He poses a rhetorical question similar to Metron's: "How can one transmit to others the infinite Aleph, which my timorous memory can scarcely contain?" As in the Swamp Thing story, the poet is scarcely able to make meaning out of what he sees. His visions through the aleph comprise the multitudinous knowledge of the entire world, yet his poetry stinks. The author of *Swamp Thing* #62, Rick Veitch, at once pays homage to Borges and goes for broke in his first issue as lead writer.

The line of influence can be traced back even further. This time it leads to a short story by the father of modern science fiction. In the afterword to his 1949 short story collection in which "The Aleph" appears, Borges makes note of the influence of a specific H.G. Wells story, "The Crystal Egg," which was published in 1897. In this story, the cantankerous owner of a London antique shop, a Mr. Cave, is reluctant to sell an egg-shaped crystal.

He acquired it by no special means in a larger lot of miscellany, and had been displaying it in the shopfront window. To the bafflement of his wife and family, the crystal egg disappears one day. As it turns out, the shop owner has hidden it himself. This is no ordinary crystal. One night, a speck of light within the crystal catches Mr. Cave's attention. He discovers that, when gazing into the egg from a certain angle, he sees a literally alien landscape of flying creatures and towering edifices. After noticing the patterns of stars in the extraterrestrial sky, he consults astronomical data with a friend and ultimately realizes that he is seeing the planet Mars. Furthermore, it seems as though there are also identical crystal eggs on Mars and that the inhabitants of that planet can see through them and into the tiny 1890's London antique shop. Presumably, all the crystal eggs can be used as communication devices, acting as windows across space. According to the story, "the terrestrial crystal must have been--possibly at some remote date—sent hither from that planet, in order to give the Martians a near view of our affairs."

Although the power of Wells' crystal egg differs from that of Borges' aleph, it is not difficult to see their relationship. In each example, a point of light gives way to spectacles beyond the imagination. *Swamp Thing* #62, published in 1987, is a noteworthy contribution to the lore of mind-expanding visions in fiction. Another popular example that readers may be familiar with is the palantir stones of J.R.R. Tolkien's Middle Earth, otherwise known as the Stones of Seeing. The craving and need to see beyond what is possible is common among the annals of science fiction, fantasy, and comic books.

Crystal-gazing, scrying, and mediumship also figured strongly in the real-world occult subculture of H.G. Wells' London. Whatever the origins of this deep desire to see into parallel worlds or to gain the wealth of all knowledge, the readership of science fiction, fantasy, and comics can be gratified. In essence, these works of literature themselves serve as our own alephs. These are the stories from which we make our own meanings.

Sources

Borges, Jorge Luis. *The Aleph and Other Stories.* Trans. Andrew Hurley. New York: Penguin, 2000.

Moore, Alan and Rick Veitch, et al. *Saga of the Swamp Thing: Book Six.* New York: DC Comics, 2011.

Wells, H.G. *Selected Stories of H.G. Wells.* Ed. Ursula K. Le Guin. New York: Modern Library, 2004.

Part II

The Writhing Discord of Utter Chaos

A Great Old One is Born

The opening page of *Swamp Thing* #8, published in 1974, presents a "certain mossy man-brute" shambling through a snowy wood. While wandering he will discover an injured old man inside a cave. Guarding this den, however, is a fierce grizzly bear. The violent clash between monsters that ensues is emblematic of the unnatural encroaching upon the natural, a chaotic event disrupting an environment of order.

Len Wein, the writer of this classic story, here establishes the conflict that imbues the Swamp Thing universe. The continuous struggle between opposing elements is the requisite stuff of comic book storytelling. Readers of issue #8 are subsequently met with a particular breed of cosmic horror.

On that same opening page, the story's title is displayed in blood red: "The Lurker in Tunnel 13!" That title is a reference to both H.P. Lovecraft's 1922 short story "The Lurking Fear" and August Derleth's 1945 novel *The Lurker at the Threshold*. The latter was composed from fragments of Lovecraft's unpublished writings. It should also be noted that the opening scene of issue #8 is reminiscent of an early Lovecraft story called "The Beast in the Cave," which shows how human fears are provoked by the dark spaces within the earth and the mysteries that may lie dormant among them. In fact, this idea is the basis of Lovecraft's Old Ones, a pantheon of ancient deities who lie in sleep within the earth, only to be temporarily reawakened by the occasional unfortunate mortal.

After Swamp Thing defeats the grizzly bear, the dying old man in the cave goes on to relate the woeful tale of the nearby town from which he hails. It once was a place that was "rich in coal and precious ores," but the town of Perdition's citizens began to flee as the natural resources dwindled. He goes on: "There wasn't any natural way to restore the mines. . . so my pappy he started checking into unnatural ways. . . the occult and the supernatural." His father apparently had summoned an Old One to wakefulness, and, after having been seen carrying mysterious books into the mine was never seen again. The old man, now through with his tale, dies. Swamp Thing carries his body into town, where its citizens lure him into the mines as a gift to their god: M'Nagalah. As the generations passed, the people of Perdition had become a cult that was now servile to the power of this horrid mass of tissue and tentacle, nastily illustrated by the great Bernie Wrightson.

With this story, Len Wein created his own contribution to the Cthulhu Mythos. According to M'Nagalah himself, his consciousness has permeated and influenced the world's evolutionary changes since time immemorial. It decreed the birth of earthly life out of the primordial soup, bestowed humanity with the capacity for "mindless violence," and finally touched the minds of writers such as Edgar Allan Poe, Ambrose Bierce, and H.P. Lovecraft. This allusion to these writers further strengthens Lovecraft's impact on the ideas in this story. The reach of M'Nagalah does not stop at this bronze age comic, however. What follows is a guide through some notable appearances of Wein's creation, which took on a life of its own through some legendary writers and artists in both comics and prose fiction.

The Disciples of Cthulhu

The first Cthulhu Mythos anthology, the one that started it all, was *Tales of the Cthulhu Mythos,* published in 1969 by the fabled Arkham House. This seminal volume was the introduction of many new writers into the Cthulhu Mythos, a term invented by the book's editor, August Derleth, who also contributed his own story to the collection. Visionary writers such as Robert E. Howard, creator of Conan the Cimmerian, appear alongside the weird fantasist Clark Ashton Smith. Horror writer Ramsey Campbell contributed the story "Cold Print," which includes the first appearance of Y'Golonac, an Old One whose main interests are the perversion and depravity found in forbidden books. Campbell would later write the forward to the first volume of Alan Moore's *Saga of the Swamp Thing* collection in 1987.

Campbell also wrote a story for the 1976 anthology *The Disciples of Cthulhu* called "The Tugging." In this story, a man's strange dreams haunt his waking life, until he finally tracks down their source in the antique remnants of a secret cult that had communed with M'Nagalah. The Old One is described as "a tentacled mass of what looked like bloated entrails and eyes," which perfectly describes the artwork of Bernie Wrightson in *Swamp Thing* #8. The man's tormented dreams also feature the ancient sunken city of R'lyeh, where Cthulhu himself lies dreaming. The vast encompassing power of the secret cult, it seems, had been one to be reckoned with. To his horror, the protagonist realizes that the pull of M'Nagalah, or the tugging, reaches deep within his consciousness. The original disciples of M'Nagalah, he discovers, were his own ancestors.

Challengers of the Unknown

The villainy of M'Nagalah next appears in a wild three-issue story arc in *Challengers of the Unknown* from 1977. In issue #81, the Challengers confront Multi-Man, a seemingly immortal figure bent on world domination. Early in the issue, the United Nations tests a nuclear weapon, a scene which no doubt preyed upon the anxieties of an American readership in an increasingly unstable world.

This was a fear that Multi-Man would try to exploit. Challenger Prof Haley, during an effort to dismantle Multi-Man's destructive plans, is instead himself thwarted, captured, and rendered comatose. The next issue continues the story with a short chapter entitled "The Lurker Below," a direct allusion to the Len Wein story, as well as to those earlier lurkers who influenced him. As it happens, the doctor who turns out to treat the insensate Prof Haley is no other than Heathcliff Monroe, a descendant of Malcomb Monroe, author of the occult book *Visions of a Dead Priest.* It was Heathcliff's ancestors, as he tells it himself, who communed with "Eternal" M'Nagalah, up to the point when Swamp Thing escaped its grasp (which is the premise of *Swamp Thing* #8).

The language of this story arc, written by Gerry Conway, is evocative of Lovecraft's writing. Case in point: "the fury of matter and energy twist to shapes beyond the range of nature itself." Also, the subtitle of issue #82 is "A journey into the unimaginable." The instability of physics and the incomprehensibility of the universe are perennial themes in Lovecraft's work. Before the final confrontation, two Challengers discover the home library of Dr. Monroe, where they find *Visions of a Dead Priest,* as well as books by the obscure authors "Von Junzt. . . Abdul Alhazred. . . Prinn." These are the authors of occult books in the Cthulhu Mythos, specifically *Nameless Cults, The Necronomicon,* and *De Vermis Mysteriis.* In the end, M'Nagalah, "the fungoid poison of a monster," is quashed by Swamp Thing, whom the Challengers enlisted. At his own demise, the Old One screams, "You dare not disrupt me again!"

The Books of Magic

The Books of Magic, a four-issue Sandman Universe series written by Neil Gaiman, is a journey into myth, folklore, and arcane history. Early in the tale, published in 1990-1991, a boy named Timothy is shown a great city in the sea, echoing a symbol which appears throughout the cycle of connected Cthulhu Mythos literature. According to an ancient magician that he meets in the mystical world beyond our own, the city is "a symbol of the Art." Timothy's guide in the first issue, the Phantom Stranger, gives him a lesson in esoteric history and culture. In the second issue, John Constantine introduces young Timothy to the figures at play beyond the veil of our normal reality, as well as the obscure machinations of the underworld. Along the way, Timothy and Constantine meet Dr. Fate, who insists that the universe is divided into the forces of order and chaos, "forever contending for dominance." He goes on, "Life is something that occurs in the interface, not in the writhing discord of utter chaos."

Constantine believes that in truth the universe is far too complex to be broken down so simply. Dr. Fate's description, however, is an apt representation of M'Nagalah, whose writhing tentacled mass appears during an epic battle in one of many possible futures we see in the final issue of *The Books of Magic.* Now accompanied by unpredictable Mister E, Timothy listens to him explain how M'Nagalah, the Great God Cancer, along with his hordes, will attempt to consume all of existence. Engaged in the battle are figures such as The Spectre, Zatanna, the demon Etrigan, and more.

Daughter of Swamp Thing Tefe' Holland, now an Earth sprite, is glimpsed in the battle and regarded as "amazing" by Timothy. He also shockingly sees his future self, fighting on the side of discord. Neil Gaiman's effective inclusion of M'Nagalah shows the impact that Len Wein's creation has had in the Cthulhu Mythos, and in comics especially.

The Trenchcoat Brigade

"What M'Nagalah wants, he simply takes." This is the troubling general assessment made of the Cancer-God, as he is referred to in *The Trenchcoat Brigade*, the four-issue Vertigo series from 1999. The reunited team of Constantine, Phantom Stranger, Dr. Occult, and Mister E encounter the wretched entity M'Nagalah in a future where he has consumed most of humanity and civilization. The distortion of time and the navigation of possible futures is a recurring theme in the stories of these four magicians, who, unlike the superheroes of the world work within the abstract vortices of space and time. M'Nagalah had been summoned by a 17th-century young woman whose flesh becomes possessed by him. As M'Nagalah slowly becomes one with her flesh and spirit, she becomes immortal yet trapped by the Cancer-God's carnal grasp.

The concept of order vs. chaos in the universe is once again explored in *The Trenchcoat Brigade*. In essence, M'Nagalah represents a literal cancer, a "corrupter and devourer of flesh," as intoned by the Phantom Stranger. Mister E calls M'Nagalah "the bane of all worlds," for what more frighteningly disrupts order than cancer itself?

We learn that M'Nagalah derives power from his victims by "absorbing the order of their flesh into the chaos of his own." Notably, an occult book also plays a role in this story, as the 17th-century young woman develops into a sorceress with *The Book of Ending,* whose cover looks conspicuously like the flesh of M'Nagalah. Contrasting with this grimoire is *The Holy Bible,* which appears in a flashback of Mister E's turbulent childhood. His domineering father, who revered the Bible, was in actuality an abusive man who traumatized the young Eric and ultimately blinds him. Here we have two books of knowledge misused, suggesting that order and chaos are two sides of the same coin depending on how the knowledge is respected and employed. In the end, Mister E sacrifices himself in order to satiate M'Nagalah and thus save the future from disaster.

The All-New Atom

The next two highlighted appearances of M'Nagalah were in series written by Gail Simone, who carries on the Cthulhu Mythos legacy of creators Wein and Wrightson. In *The All-New Atom,* which premiered in 2006, young Dr. Ryan Choi carries on the legacy of his predecessor Ray Palmer as the new Atom. Taking a position as an Ivy University particle physics professor, Choi is quickly thrust into a conflict between "chaos and order, faith and reason, magic and science." On the side of order, reason, and science is a technologically-advanced alien race with an insectoid disposition. At the helm of chaos, faith, and magic is of course our disagreeable undulating blob M'Nagalah. Swamp Thing makes a brief, shadowy appearance in a flashback told by M'Nagalah.

Later, an allusion to Swamp Thing #8 is made in the title of the drive-thru movie called *The Terror of Tunnel Thirteen*. In issue #2, M'Nagalah calls himself "the face and fountain of all human knowledge."

The limit of human knowledge is a theme explored in this series, especially in conversation among Choi's tight-knit group of new friends, the brilliant professors of the university physics department. The Atom's ability to change size, and the dangerous plight that continually presents itself as a result, is cleverly reinforced with text boxes inserted throughout the story. For example, in a scene wherein the Atom's new invention acts dangerously out of control, in contrast to early testing, there appears this quote from Stephen Hawking: "Our ability to predict the future is severely limited by the complexity of the equations, and the fact that they often have a property called chaos." This unpredictable element of Chaos is represented by M'Nagalah, whose aggression is eventually suppressed when the Atom destroys the alien army by using his intellect instead of pure force. Other figures such as Carl Sagan, Albert Einstein, and Isaac Asimov lend their wisdom and insight in the commentary that parallels the narrative. Even Dr. Alec Holland is quoted, with an ironic quip from Len Wein's story "Dark Genesis," from *Swamp Thing* #1: "Seems almost a shame we're not building a monster."

The Secret Six

M'Nagalah lastly rears his vast amorphous head in the "House of Strangers" story arc, which begins with *The Secret Six* #7, a 2015 comic written by Gail Simone. The esoteric cast of characters begins to realize that "the arcane network is decaying," meaning that some unknown force is effectually sucking the element of magic totally out of existence. This would be a crisis, since it will leave the world defenseless against entities such as the Great Old Ones and the Outer Gods. Swamp Thing and Deadman are shown completely emaciated and bereft of power.

Meanwhile, the Children of Arion, a cult that claims to be the "true Atlanteans," attempt to take advantage of the Secret Six, telling them that they must find and destroy the White Gate, which provides an Earthen force field that was erected in ancient times by the Atlantean wizard Arion. This is the only way that Secret Six member Black Alice will survive, according to the Children of Arion, since it is she who is unintentionally sponging all the power of magic.

Amidst this maelstrom of action, Aquaman appears to defend his Atlantean home from the Secret Six, who wish to destroy the White Gate, a pillar of which is located at Atlantis. They do eventually succeed, which awakens M'Nagalah, who is holding the townspeople of Perdition in mental captivity. The following sequence, wherein the Secret Six go to Perdition seeking another pillar of the White Gate, comes full circle to *Swamp Thing* #8. As the team beholds the seething mass that is M'Nagalah, he says, "the Elder Gods bless your mission. Take the column and destroy it." Only then will he have the capability to fully subsume himself in the earth and consume all (which is what does happen in the alternate future of *The Trenchcoat Brigade).*

M'Nagalah is duped by the Secret Six and apparently killed, for he states, "Go. M'Nagalah is dying." A brutal and perverse ending is insinuated, moreover, as the famished townspeople of Perdition approach M'Nagalah for revenge with bared teeth and hungry mouths.

The Mythos Endures

While the apparent demise of M'Nagalah occurs in *The Secret Six* #9, writer Gail Simone introduces her own Great Old One in the very next issue. Thrumm, as he is called, is a Dark Giant who has existed since time immemorial, and the weakening of the White Gate has hastened his return. What tools of magic will each side of the impending conflict employ? The occult knowledge contained within Lovecraft's fictional magnum opus, *The Necronomicon,* works as a tool for tipping the cosmic scales toward its handler. In addition to its appearance in *Challengers of the Unknown, The Necronomicon* plays a significant role in Nancy A. Collins' *Swamp Thing* #114. The enigmatic book can also be glimpsed in the stacks of Sargon the Sorcerer's personal library in Mark Millar's *Swamp Thing* #148. Thanks to the cosmic horror legacy of Len Wein and Bernie Wrightson, the Cthulhu Mythos has endured throughout the storied pages of a certain mossy man-brute, the Avatar of The Green.

What conveys a particularly strong type of fear is that Lovecraft's cosmic deities are not necessarily evil, to be exact. They are actually something far more horrifying—they are *indifferent*. It is a universe of absolute indifference that confronts humanity, while the perceived balance of order and chaos is arbitrary and indiscriminate. Whenever there exists a semblance of order restored to the universe, it seems, an agent of chaos turns up. As much as we might like to think that the Good will prevail and remain, the continual primeval battle with Evil goes on. The ancient archetypes are as strong as ever, and the real-life fears and anxieties amidst the continual battle are accordingly reflected in our comics and horror storytelling.

ACKNOWLEDGEMENTS

Thank you to the editors, publishers, and writers who have shown me nothing but support and encouragement. Especially, these are Gabriel McCaughry, John Boylan, Maria J. Perez Cuervo, Nathaniel Winter-Hebert, Jon Padgett, Clint Marsh, Lizbeth Poirier, John Chrostek, and Mark Ryan.

Thank you to C.F. Page for the cover blurb.

Special thanks to Bart Gibbons, who kindly proofread and edited my essays in their early drafts.

I owe everything to my parents, Fina and Aleco. Immense gratitude for their lifetime support of me and all my endeavors.

Extra special thanks to Alejandra, Viviana, and Rebecca. My universe at home.

PUBLICATION HISTORY

"And Yet It Deviated" originally appeared in *Cold Signal Magazine*, issue 1

"The Abyss of all Being" originally appeared in *Hellebore*, issue 5

"Endless Forms Most Beautiful" appears in *Fiddler's Green Peculiar Parish Magazine*, issue 9

"Florilegium Stellarum" originally appeared in Anathema Publishing's *A Wayfarer's Hearth*

A version of "The Path of the Labyrinth" originally appeared in *Hellebore*, issue 7

"No Longer Remotely Human" originally appeared in *Vastarien*, Volume 5, Issue 2

"To Ravish & Intoxicate" originally appeared in Anathema Publishing's *Seeds of Ares*

"Life's But a Poor Player" originally published online by the Yale National Initiative

"All of Infinity Within One Gigantic Instant" originally appeared in *Holland Files*, issue 4

"The Writhing Discord of Utter Chaos" originally appeared in *Holland Files*, issue 6

"Phantom Lands" originally appeared in *Fantomes*, issue 2

"Stone Secrets of the Great Lakes" originally appeared in *Myth & Lore*, issue 5

About the Author

Aleco Julius is a teacher, writer of fiction and nonfiction, and book collector. His work has appeared in various publications, including *Vastarien, Seeds of Ares, A Wayfarer's Hearth, Hellebore, Cold Signal Magazine, Holland Files, Fiddler's Green, Anterior Skies, Myth & Lore, Dark Matter Magazine,* and *Fantomes.* He is a member of the Horror Writers Association.

Reach him on Instagram: @dagger_of_the_mind, and Twitter: @DaggerMind.

He lives in Chicago, where he is often found in the pit at a crushing doom metal show.

www.ingramcontent.com/pod-product-compliance
Lightning Source LLC
Chambersburg PA
CBHW072139300726
48975CB00003B/1122